A Life of Miracles

AN AUTOBIOGRAPHY

DR. MYNOR VARGAS

A LIFE OF MIRACLES - Autobiography

Author, Writer and Protagonist: Dr. Mynor A. Vargas, Ph.D.
Editor: Lic. M.A. Victor Suchite
Revision: Edin Yaxcal
Translation to English: Alan Crookham
Revision in English: Yeral Ogando
Last Revision in English: Brenda Archila
Lexis and Terminology Adjustments: Pastor Sheyna Vargas
Diagramming and Design: Luis Juarez
Lithography: Punto Creativo Editorial - Cesar Reyes

ISBN-13:9781479207800

IMDESA Internacional
Dr. Mynor Vargas
P.O. Box 29267
Providence, RI 02909

mynor1@aol.com
www.ShalomRI.com
www.ChaplainFederation.com
www.Mynor.com

Contents

Introduction..v

Prologue ix

CHAPTER 1. From My Mother's Womb 1

CHAPTER 2. Miracles in My Childhood..........................19

CHAPTER 3. The Biggest Miracle....................................31

CHAPTER 4. Miracles in the Air 43

CHAPTER 5. Financial Miracles 91

CHAPTER 6. Little BIG Miracles.................................... 113

CHAPTER 7. The Miracle of Living Like a
Millionaire, Without Being a Millionaire 145

CHAPTER 8. A BIG Title for a Small Servant...............171

Introduction

The Bible is full of miracles! It couldn't be any other way because our God is big and powerful! Therefore, I begin my autobiography by affirming that **I believe in miracles** as surely as I believe in God and in the Sacred Scriptures. So my dear reader, I invite you to fill yourself with faith, and venture to read and believe in miracles. The word "miracle" has been defined in many ways by theologians and dictionaries. Personally, I define a miracle as "An event performed by God outside the limits of natural law, with the purpose of supporting his Word or benefiting one or several people."

Let us break down this concept a little into three parts:

1. "An event performed by God." This should be clarified because there are also miracles realized by Satan and his followers. Let us remember, for example, when Moses asked Aaron to cast his staff before Pharaoh for it to transform into a serpent. Upon seeing that powerful act, Pharaoh proceeded to call wise men and sorcerers who did the same. However, the Bible clearly states: *"...but Aaron's rod swallowed up their rods."* This means that Satan is an imitator or forger of miracles, but his limited power will never exceed the infinite power of God. Therefore, the miracles I will speak of are miracles performed by the powerful hand of God.

2. "Outside the limits of natural law." If that were not the case, it would not be a miracle, because it is something supernatural. Something outside of natural limits, which has to do with divine intervention in human affairs. A miracle is also something unusual. It is not something that happens every day. I have experienced several miracles myself that you will come to know as you read on. They are tremendously special events, which are unusual or exceptional, as they are the exception and not the rule. Miracles are events that take place in the natural world, by supernatural power. There are four Greek words used in the Bible for miracles: *[Semeion]* sign, *[Erga]* works, *[Dunameis]* powerful works, and *[Terata]* wonders. What can I say about this? Considering that miracles do not have logical or material explanations since they occur outside of natural laws, man cannot take the credit for them.

3. "With the purpose of reinforcing his Word or benefiting one or several persons." A miracle, then, may be intended to legitimize the Word of God. That is to say, authenticate the message of the Messenger. Many times God did a miracle to reinforce his Word. But God can also work a miracle to benefit one or several persons. Jesus lived a life of miracles. In the four canonical gospels nearly 40 miracles performed by Jesus are recorded. Some of them reinforced his Word and confirmed his deity (when he calmed the storm, Matthew 8:23-27 or when he cursed the fig tree, Matthew 21:18-22). Other miracles benefited one or several persons (the healing of the woman with the issue of blood, Mark 5:25-35, the multiplication of the bread and fish, Luke 9:10-17).

Of course, there were many more miracles and works done by Jesus that are not recorded. The Apostle John explains in this way *"Jesus did many other things as well.*

If every one of them were written down, I suppose that even the whole world would not have room for the books that would be written. Amen (John 21:25). The life of Jesus was Holy and wonderful. He is our model in every area. He is our Redeemer and our Master. His life inspires our life. He came to give us eternal life and abundant life while we live here on earth. *"...I am come that they might have life, and that they might have it more abundantly"* (John 10:10). Personally, I find this promise to be suitable. These words have become a reality in my life, I have life abundantly and I have experienced "A Life of Miracles."

I am convinced that my existence is a living miracle supernaturally wrought by God, with the purpose that not only I would benefit, but that others would benefit as well. Prepare yourself to see part of my life through story form, especially those moments where I personally know I have experienced the miraculous hand of God operating in my favor. Prepare to know a true adventure of faith. I pray it will infect you with hope. Prepare yourself as well to live, "A Life of Miracles."

The Author.

Prologue

There is nothing God does not know (he is Omniscient), there is no place God does not exist (he is Omnipresent) and there is nothing God cannot do (he is Omnipotent). Our wonderful God is All Powerful. That is one of his characteristics, particularities, or attributes, which is why he is capable of working miracles. Now, God does not exercise power just to impress or put on a show. When a miracle occurs and the supernatural power of God is manifested, it always goes hand in hand with his sovereign will. Jesus knew this truth! When he was suffering in the garden of Gethsemane he prayed to the Father. Humanly speaking Jesus did not want to die on the cross. It wasn't pleasant to think of those nails piercing his hands and feet, or that crown of thorns embedded in his forehead. He knew that God could stop it, he could send a legion of his angels and intervene, but he asked that not his will be done, but the Father's (see Mark 14:35-36). The Omnipotence of God cannot be separated from his Sovereignty, which means that any believer can receive the power of God, and that must be connected to his will.

The life of Mynor Vargas really is "A Life of Miracles", because this servant of the Lord Jesus Christ, lives connected to his holy will and purpose. Twenty six years ago, he led me to Jesus Christ and evangelized a group of my friends who lived completely separated from God. That is to say, his love for the Lord and his willingness to serve him has been around for several decades. I am an eyewitness to this since then we have been inseparable colleagues in ministry. Even though we currently live in different countries, we see each other several times a year and maintain constant communication. I know he is a man of faith and is very dynamic. From there, with an entrepreneurial spirit he has been a producer of Radio and Television programs, Author of newspaper articles and of several books, Advisor to important ministries, Trainer and Certifier of hundreds of chaplains around the world, International Speaker, Evangelist in massive meetings, Founder of a prominent Consortium of Churches, as well as Crown University in New England, Pastor of Shalom Auditorium in the city of Providence, RI, in the United States of America, among other ministerial projects. This untiring traveler, exemplary husband, responsible father, and holder of several doctorates, has experienced the hand of God working in his life from the time before he was even born.

You have in your hands a book that will not only tell you the special way in which God has manifested miraculously on repeated occasions in the life of one of his servants, but it will also inspire you in your life. It will fill you with faith. It will challenge you and captivate you. I assure you that once you begin reading this work, you will not put it down until you have finished it. The interesting, strange, funny, and incredible stories will capture your whole attention. Mynor has the blessing of feeling the power of God, but also to describe his life in a particular way that is entertaining, and with a great sense of humor.

This is not just another biography, these are the experiences of someone who has learned that the power of God is unlimited, and it's more important than economic power or the political power that some hold in this world. To be honest, that kind of power does not even remotely compare to the Omnipotence of God. Generally our finite minds cannot comprehend the infinite power of God. This book will help us understand it a little bit more.

However, I must clarify that in most instances there are two important elements needed to produce a miracle, especially when the believer sees the benefits: 1) The power of God; 2) the faith of the Christian. Jesus many times repeated the phrase, "your faith has saved you." For example, the woman with the hemorrhage that lasted twelve years, Jesus said to her: *"Daughter, thy faith hath made thee whole; go in peace, and be whole of thy plague"* (Mark 5:34). I am reminded that in that moment, Jesus was walking beside Jairus, the disciples, and a multitude of curious people on the way to Jairus' house, with the purpose of praying for his daughter who was dying. The Lord did not have plans to heal that woman who little by little opened a way through the multitude, with the goal of touching the hem of Jesus' robe. According to the law she was unclean (Leviticus 15:19-33), therefore, it was prohibited for her to touch someone who was clean. She thought that simply touching Jesus' robe was sufficient to be healed. Surely she did not believe that there was something magical in the Lord's robe. But there was no other option left and she had faith that if she could touch it, healing power would come out from him. In fact, that is exactly what happened, because *"Jesus, immediately knowing in himself that virtue had gone out of him, turned him about in the press, and said, Who touched my clothes?"* (Mark 5:30). That means, that the power which healed her, came out of Jesus and not his robes. So it was the faith of the woman, united with the power of God that produced the miracle.

I explain this because the level of faith that you and I have is key in the intervention of God in our lives.

God has intervened miraculously in the life of my friend and brother Mynor Vargas, precisely because of his elevated level of faith.

I invite you to get comfortable on a good sofa, prepare a good cup of coffee, or the drink of your choice, and start this interesting read that will motivate you to be an entrepreneur for the glory of God. I was the first of thousands of readers that will be filled with faith through this important work.

Lic. M.A. Victor Súchite
Pastor of East Nazareth Church in Guatemala

1

FROM MY
MOTHER'S WOMB

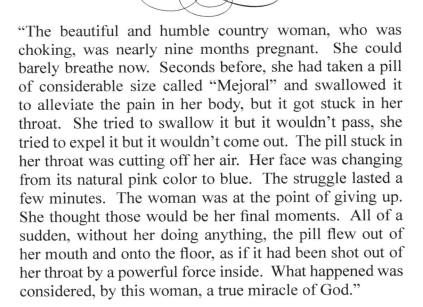

"The beautiful and humble country woman, who was choking, was nearly nine months pregnant. She could barely breathe now. Seconds before, she had taken a pill of considerable size called "Mejoral" and swallowed it to alleviate the pain in her body, but it got stuck in her throat. She tried to swallow it but it wouldn't pass, she tried to expel it but it wouldn't come out. The pill stuck in her throat was cutting off her air. Her face was changing from its natural pink color to blue. The struggle lasted a few minutes. The woman was at the point of giving up. She thought those would be her final moments. All of a sudden, without her doing anything, the pill flew out of her mouth and onto the floor, as if it had been shot out of her throat by a powerful force inside. What happened was considered, by this woman, a true miracle of God."

The story you just read is one that my mother told me over and over again when I was a child, a youth, and even an adult. My older sister Maria Magdalena Vargas Leon, who we lovingly call Magda, has done the same. The beautiful country woman was my own mother Virgilia Belarmina Vargas Oliva (Mama Mina) and the child who was in her womb, was me. I say she was beautiful, but not only physically, also because my mother had a great

personality. Those who knew her can confirm this. She
was very loving and always giving advice to those who
visited her. I say she was a country woman because my
parents were from the country side, or rural area. Also,
in the era that I was born, they lived on a humble piece
of a ranch on a remote mountain between Guatemala and
Honduras. I also believe that the event was a miracle,
because that is how my mother interpreted it, being that I
was not an eyewitness to it, but I was a direct beneficiary.
She told me that if God had not performed a miracle,
that pill would have killed her, and as a result, me as
well. I have no doubt that in the goodness of God and
his blessing for my life, it was laid in his eternal plans
that neither my mother nor I would die in that event.
My mother was not just a kind of spiritual leader in my
life, who led me to Christ and advised me numerous
times, but also during all her life she spoke about Christ
to hundreds of people. Therefore, I understand that the
miracle was not just to preserve my life in her womb, but
also to use her as a useful instrument in the hands of God
.

What is certain is that I, like David, can say before all
and before God, *"For thou hast possessed my reins: thou
hast covered me in my mother's womb. I will praise thee;
for I am fearfully and wonderfully made: marvelous are
thy works; and that my soul knoweth right well."* (Psalm
139:13-14). I am in agreement one hundred percent
with the psalmist: I am mouth agape, filled with wonder,
surprise, and impressed when I observe the work of God
in my life, as much in my present life, as well as within
my mother's womb. I also proclaim together with Isaiah:
*"Listen, O isles, unto me; and hearken, ye people, from
far; The LORD hath called me from the womb; from the
bowels of my mother hath he made mention of my name"*
(Isaiah 49:1). Just as the prophet announced, to everyone
he could, the news of the Redeemer who was to come,

because God called him or predestined him to a job before he was born; I am convinced of my call to salvation and to ministry from my mother's womb. That is why I seek the best way to personally communicate to the world in conferences, evangelistic crusades, by radio, by internet, etc., the message of salvation by faith in Christ by the grace of God. Of course, I don't deserve it, and I am not worthy of it. Jeremiah rejected for a moment this privilege and made excuses before God. However, the Lord confirmed it: *"Before I formed thee in the belly I knew thee; and before thou camest forth out of the womb I sanctified thee, and I ordained thee a prophet unto the nations."* (Jeremiah 1:5) In that same way I deduce that God not only saved me miraculously in the womb of my mother, but also separated me, and set me apart and sanctified me to carry out His work. It is not my work, but His. Finally, I believe that just as Paul was destined to apostolic ministry, God has also destined me to said ministry through the Shalom International Church Consortium, through which I can say together with the Great Apostle: *"But when it pleased God, who separated me from my mother's womb, and called me by his grace, To reveal his Son in me, that I might preach him among the heathen..."* (Galatians 1:15-16).

IMPORTANT HISTORY

Let me inform you: The contemporary political history of Guatemala began in 1954, a year in which the Government of Jacobo Arbenz Guzman (after several years of democratic attempts and social reforms), was overthrown by a military strike supported by the CIA. Afterward several oppressive military governments presided over the country until the general elections of 1985, in which Vinicio Cerezo, the leader of the Christian Democratic Party was chosen as the first civil President.   So when I was born, Guatemala was governed by the admired Coronel Enrique Peralta Azurdia, who overthrew General Ydigoras Fuentes through a coup, rising to be President on April 1st 1963 and ceding that burden on July 1st 1966 to Julio Cesar Montenegro. In his time, he was the second government of the revolution, a Constituent Assembly passed the new constitution of the country in 1965, through which the presidential period was reduced from six to four years. Also, employees were given a yearly bonus of one month's work for the first time. On the other hand the government of Peralta Azurdia was the one that decreed the Civil Code, the Procedural Civil and Merchant Code, the Emission Law of Thought and the Law of Public Order, with others. Peralta retired from politics some time later and moved to the city of Miami, Florida, U.S.A., where he died in 1997 .

Although I was born on a mountain between Guatemala and Honduras, on the other side of the Motagua River, I am Guatemalan, as were my parents. My father was: Jose Facundo Vargas Morales (Papa Cundo) and was from the village of Llano Verde, Municipality of Rio Hondo, Department of Zacapa, Guatemala. My mother was Virgilia Belarmina Oliva Roldan de Vargas, and was born in the village of Mal Paso, Municipality of Rio Hondo, Department of Zacapa, Guatemala.   However, they registered my birth in Los Amates, Izabal, Guatemala; where they received my birth certificate.

MIRACULOUS BIRTH

In that remote border area where I was born, there was no hospital, or clinics, and certainly no private sanatoriums. On that same ranch where my parents lived, right there, I was born. My mother was not attended to by a doctor,

or even a nurse, but by a midwife. I do not intend to
exaggerate when I say that my birth was a miraculous one
that 7th of August 1964. Judge for yourself beloved reader:
When I was born, the midwife, my mother, and my sister
Magda were present, and were surprised by my weight.
They used a roman scale to weigh me, which marked 14
pounds and 8 ounces. I was a huge baby. Practically
speaking I was double the weight of a normal baby when
it is born. In very rare cases there have been children
born that have weighed up to 19 and 22 pounds, which
is the average weight for a child of six months. Today
when a child of that size is born, the mother undergoes
a caesarian section, and can depend on a surgeon with a
team of doctors, anesthesiologists, hygienic conditions,
etc. However, there, where I was born, there were no
more than a few cloths soaking in water in a pewter pot,
which was over a fire. If something were to go wrong,
the worst would have been expected. Any doctor can
confirm that just as with a premature birth, the life of an
underweight child runs a risk; a birth where a baby weighs
too much or its position in the moment of giving birth is
incorrect, the life of the mother and especially the child is
in grave danger. This information was confirmed to us by
Dr. Percy Jacobs, a pediatrician with more than 40 years
of experience in Guatemala.

Despite those dangers, mine was a completely natural
birth. There was no medical assistance or forceps. There
were also no physical lesions on the mother or child, at
the moment of delivery. There was no subconjunctival
hemorrhage (rupture of small blood vessels in the babies'
eyes). There were no fractures or tumors, which are
also possible risks. There was perfect dilation, perfect
embedding, and a good progressive descent of the
baby through the birth canal and an excellent expulsion
of the baby until the complete exit of the placenta and

membranes. There were no professional hands, but the hand of the Divine Doctor was present. Mama Mina and I were safe and sound, to live a long life filled with beautiful blessings. My mother, who lived 86 years before being called to the presence of the Lord, used to tell me on repeated occasions: "Oh son! What danger we lived on that mountain, what risks son, with me giving birth to you under such precarious circumstances." Because of all of that, I am convinced that mine was a miraculous birth.

MY FIRST GALE STORM

In my life diverse winds and storms have come against me; however my first literal storm happened when I was only two months old. Allow me to do an analysis of living conditions in Guatemala City and in the rest of the country before I explain what happened on that mountain. In the 60's (when I was born), the upper class abandoned the center of the city and moved to zones 9 and 10, extending later into zones 13 and 14. Later, when the city continued expanding they sought to reside in the southeast of the city, or the current zone 15. As the city was growing the main exits of the metropolis were roads which were built into various bridges to cross the deep ravines. These roads formed a ring to unite at the arteries of the Atlantic and Pacific. After that they created other colonies for the middle class in zones 6, 7, 11, 12 and 18; the poor lived in ravines, vacant land, settlements and rooms for rent in zones 3, 4, 5, 6 and 8. All this happened in the city, while we were not living in a village, or a municipality, much less within a department head, but on a distant mountain, separated from civilization. We also didn't live in luxurious houses or in rooms for rent like some of our countrymen in the city. We lived on a simple straw ranch behind the Motagua River. This is where we found

ourselves when I was two months old. It was at that time
when a severe cyclonic storm, or tropical depression,
passed over those lands and caused disasters (at least in
our case). Because it happened in 1964, and because we
could not depend on advanced technology in those days,
nobody communicated anything to anyone and even less
to those in remote places. In celebration of my birth
my parents gave a down payment to a truck driver (Don
Arnoldo) who used to travel to the city. This money was
to be used to buy our family a radio transmitter. What a
party we had at home! (that is to say, in our old ranch), at
the end of the month when Don Arnoldo the truck driver
arrived, and in his hand was a grand yellow radio made by
Philips that used 16 "D" batteries, (the biggest ones)! The
radio was the newest model, plus it had a fine leather belt
wrapped all around it. This radio was the spokesman who
let us know that strong gale winds would hit the border of
Guatemala and Honduras, exactly where we lived.

The miracle is summed up in that my mother did not want
to leave the old ranch because she was preparing an old
pot of black beans. The whole family had taken refuge
in a house of concrete blocks which was property of
Coronel Monzon, but my mother insisted that she could
not abandon the pot of black beans. At the same time she
refused to give her two month old child to them in order
to take him to the Colonel's house (in case you forgot, the
baby was me). How did the miracle happen? From one
instant to another, my sister Magda took the baby in her
hands and my mother, seeing they were taking me, ran out
of the house in search of her newborn. This action not
only happened to save my life but also the life of Mama
Mina, because only a few minutes after she left the house
was overtaken and blown into thousands of fragments by
the powerful hurricane winds. No doubt God uses others
to save us. In that moment he used my older sister. At

times I've thought that God desired to preserve my life, in other occasions I've thought he wanted to save my mother. In the end, I have come to the conclusion that God was interested in saving us both. My mother and I have both preached the Word of God, serving others with acts of love and generosity. I am sure that I am generous because my mother was. From her I learned to give generous offerings to servants of God. From her I learned to give to those in need. My mother was the first person in the family to know the Gospel; she won for Christ, my father and all my siblings. Because of that, I am convinced that God worked a miracle to rescue her life and saved her from certain and premature death. Just as Satan wanted to end the life of Jesus when he was a child, he wanted to end mine in childhood as well, to see the plan of God truncated in the life of honorable and useful vessels.

THE SECRET KEPT FOR 45 YEARS

The Bible does not make mistakes; it is the infallible Word of God. The Sacred Scriptures affirm that, *"To every thing there is a season, and a time to every purpose under the heaven"* (Ecclesiastes 3:1). After underlining this great truth, Solomon gives some examples indicating that there is a time to be born and a time to die, to cry and laugh, etc. But in verse 7 of chapter 3 in Ecclesiastes, it adds *"time to keep silence, and a time to speak."* Permit me to open my heart and tell you, precious reader, that as I finished writing this first chapter of the autobiography you have in your hands, I discovered a secret which had not been revealed to me for 45 years. It came to light in the will of God, in the time to speak. It was my sister Trinis who told me this truth that had been hidden from me.

Before sharing it with you, and to have a clearer panorama of the issue, I want to tell you of a sad truth that is not a secret: Guatemala is a poor country. I must admit that it is a third world country. It was when I was born, and sadly continues to be that way in the XXI century. Although it is a nation that naturally possesses abundant riches, due to bad distribution of these natural riches and resources Guatemala continues in its poverty. The social inequalities are abysmal in my beloved country. Some 2% of the population of the country own 80% of the lands, which is to say, a few multimillionaire families are owners of practically the entire country. Of those, 60% live in poverty (that is to say, living on two dollars daily according to the World Bank). The average income currently is USD 1,500.00 per year, which is Q12, 000.00 in the national currency. Adding to that, 40% of the population does not know how to read or write. The same way the index of poverty, illiteracy is very high. My heart is drowned in sadness to know that there are 56,000 orphan children because of internal war and more than 5,000 children live and sleep on the streets in the capital. Fortunately, after signing a peace treaty which put an end to 36 years of civil war, there have been visible improvements in the economic aspect and the gradual progress of the country has been remarkable.

Why do I share all of this? Because I come from a family in extreme poverty as you precisely remember. I have already described to you the ranch where my parents lived with four children not including me. One more statistic: The majority of the poor people live in rural areas, close to 72%, while only 28% live in urban areas. I was born in a rural area. Rural areas are where poverty effects people the most.

Now, let me get back to the secret kept for 45 years: It was 10:37 a.m. on Friday the 23rd of April 2010, I called my sister Magda to inquire more about my birth; we talked by cell phone for 12 minutes and 23 seconds (of course, we had dialogued many times before). While Magda told me the details, my sister Trinis heard part of Magda's conversation and realized that she omitted a difficult part of the story which nobody else knew. Trinis had a secret that possibly no other member of the family knew. A story that maybe only she had heard (and maybe Magda as well), but up to that day she was not willing to reveal it. When we finished speaking on the telephone with my older sister, Trinis asked her:

"Magda, what were you speaking with Mynor about?"

She responded,

"About a book. Little Mynor is writing his autobiography, especially about his life of miracles."

It was then that Trinis said to herself, "Could now be the time to tell him the big secret?" If Magda did know it, she didn't seem very convinced of the idea of revealing it. However Trinis considered that secret to be part of my history and it was in that moment that I learned of it.

As soon as Trinis left the house, she called me on her cell phone to tell me that she heard about my project and there was something I should know. Since she studied psychology, she told me that she had psychoanalyzed me, and believed I was emotionally strong enough to hear a hard and bitter part of the story of before my birth. The call cut off in the middle of the conversation because of a bad signal, but the digital register showed that we spoke for 25 minutes and 20 seconds the first time, and 17 minutes and

56 seconds during the next time we spoke. That means we spoke for a total of 43 minutes and 16 seconds about this story which I am sharing with you.

Trinis informed be about a miracle in my life which I did not know. She assured me that it didn't show any lack of respect towards my mother by telling me, because my mother desired for someone to tell me how God preserved my life. My sister informed me that our mother told her the truth of why I weighed so much and as she told the story, my mother became very emotional. Here is the summary of my mother's story:

"The baby's weight was not normal little daughter, remember that the children of country women were not well fed. When I became pregnant with Mynor, we didn't have more than a few chickens in the yard and some herbs to eat. Your father only had two black shirts that were so thin that mosquitoes would bite him through the fabric. Your father only had one pair of pants, which he had to take off each night so that I could wash it and leave it out to dry for the morning. I only had one dress and two blouses, along with one pair of sandals, although I didn't use them because I was used to going barefoot. When I realized that I was pregnant again I was very happy to know that a new person was coming into the world, but I also thought that there would be no way to sustain another baby. All four of you were already suffering hunger; you were also barefoot and half naked. I could not accept that another child would come into the world to suffer, so I called a midwife and an herbalist to help me. The decision was very firm and certain; I did not want to see my son suffer hunger. The midwife gave me herbs so that Mynor would not be born, and she told me to drink hot bean broth every day. She continuously gave me diverse kinds of herbs and I drank lots of broths"…

Although my mother tried many times to reveal this truth to me, I did not give her the chance and she died without telling me the story. It wasn't until April 23rd, 2010 that for the first time, my sister Trinis told me the true story of my birth. I have no doubt the herbalist made a mistake, because nobody can mess with the plans of God. As much as she tried, instead of provoking a miscarriage, she **caused a giant healthy baby to be born; a super baby weighing 14 pounds and 8 ounces. To God be the glory for ages upon ages and forever, amen!** Personally, I do not have the words to express what all of this constitutes, never the less I will add that the midwife herbalist was not an ignorant woman pulling recipes out of the air. On the contrary, she was an expert who had never failed before. Other trustworthy sources have said that when she did this kind of work, she carried a cloth in one hand and a knife in the other. In the cases where the mother wanted to have the baby, she received it with the cloth, while on the contrary, SHE NEVER BEFORE FAILED TO PROVOKE A PREMATURE BIRTH… My case was the exception. There is no doubt that God cared for me and I am in the palm of his hand.

My mother never hated me. She loved me and I was the child she spoiled the most. My brothers and sisters can confirm this truth. She spoiled me until the last breath of her life. When I was a boy, it didn't matter if my brothers were watching some program on the television, or if my father was watching the news: if "Little Mynor" wanted to watch cartoons or another program, he just had to glance in that direction and that was it. Basically, I had control with just a frown, because my mother spoiled me and loved me enormously. So when I was born, my mother was joyful and said to God, **"Now you gave him to me, and you are going to sustain him."**

Trinis says that my mother confessed that I was welcomed
to the world, but her worry was that there wouldn't be the
means to feed me. But at the moment of my birth, she
loved me and God taught her a great lesson: He is the
only one who gives and takes life. In fact, it is a good
idea to clarify that in those days my mother was still not
a believer in Christ. Even with this, the reality is that
my mother is the greatest woman I have ever met in the
world. A big truth has been revealed to me, and it does
not change my opinion about her at all. Mama Mina is the
most precious woman I have ever met, the kindest, and
I will never love anyone like I do her. I understand that
poverty and ignorance can cause good people to make bad
decisions. If someone were to make a movie about my
life, I would like it to have the same title as the Hollywood
success *"Hard to Kill"* with Steven Seagal.

VISITING THE CEMETARY
WITH MY SISTER MAGDA

My sister Magda, who knows that I frequently go to the
cemetery to bring flowers and meditate for a while, and to
remember mama and papa, asked if she could go with me
one day. I immediately realized that this would be a good
opportunity to ask her if she was hiding something about
an episode in my life.

First, we went to buy eight seedlings with beautiful flowers.
Later, we went to buy a shovel to plant them together at the
grave. Before we started walking toward the cemetery we
stopped to have breakfast in a restaurant called "T's." The
conversation started without small talk or beating around
the bush; I said, "Magda, there are things you haven't told
me, including about how I almost wasn't born.

She looked at me with a fixed gaze with her eyes interrogating me on how I knew. So as to not lose time or run in circles around the subject as we usually did, I said,

"It was Trinis, and with good reason. Now you have to tell me your side of the story. What really happened?" I asked her.

My older sister confirmed that my mother suffered emotionally when she discovered she was pregnant with me. She told me that she did want me to be born, and that she loved me even in the womb, but at the same time she did not wish to have another child. This was because she was conscious of the fact that I would go through hunger and suffer in this world. Her version of the facts, were very close to the story Trinis told me, but with more details. She told me that the recipe used for the baby not to be born was very effective, and had already produced clear results with other country people. When this formula was used, it never failed, until they tried it on me. The procedure did not only consist of using herbs and black bean broth, but it also used what I call "the coup de grace." It consisted of using a pill called "quinine" (scientifically it may be quimosine, but that isn't for sure). When pregnant women took this pill, they would abort the child immediately. I did not abort with one, or two, or even several pills. Truly *"I am more than a conqueror through him that loved me"* (Romans 8:37).

Magda told me about another very sad case. A neighbor ingested the "quinine" pill. The sad result was the death not only of the child, but the mother as well. It is so sad to know that to the humble people of the mountains, as well as the wealthy in the suburbs, the devil comes *"to steal, and to kill, and to destroy."* But glory to God! Jesus came to give me *"life, and life in abundance"* (John 10:10).

As I wrote these last lines of chapter one, I did an ample and deep scientific investigation, verifying that "quinine" does exist. It is also known as "quimosine", "cinchona", and finally "quinine", along with a variety of other derivatives and compositions. It is a pill that is administered to cows in order to abort their calves when they are not wanted. The "cinchona" is a pill of rennet which causes brucellosis. **Brucellosis**, also called **Malta fever**, or **undulant fever**, is a sickness that attacks various species of mammals, one of which are humans, causing human brucellosis. In the same way it attacks other mammals, within which we find some with high economic relevance such as cattle, horses, pigs, sheep, goats and other wildlife. The causal relationship between the sickness and the organism were established by Dr. David Bruce (microbiology) in 1887.

QUININE VS. MYNOR AND BELARMINA

As you will remember, Belarmina was my mother's name. Quinine is the name of the tablet she ingested several times and I am Mynor THE ONE WHO WON! According to Wikipedia the pill is described in this way: *"The natural alkaloid quinine is a white, crystalline, with antipyretic, antimalarial and analgesic. It tastes very bitter. It is a stereoisomer of quinidine. It was the main compound used in the treatment of malaria until it was replaced by other, more effective synthetic drugs. The use of quinine in high doses can be lethal, due to an acute and fulminant pulmonary edema. At very high doses it can cause spontaneous abortion. Furthermore, quinine is considered a teratogen in category X by the U.S. FDA, which means it can cause birth defects if taken by women during pregnancy."*

Why have I detailed all of this? To help you remember that the exterminator of souls, called Satan, wanted to kill me. He, and only he, is the denigrate guilty of a crime that almost ended my life before I left the womb. Therefore, the war is on and without mercy. However, Satan or the devil is a defeated enemy. He was defeated by Christ on Calvary and is defeated by God through strength of our preaching all over the world. While we preach the Word of God and the Gospel of truth, more souls will meet Jesus and be saved, and the rebellious cherubim of darkness who is the father of hell itself, will be ashamed.

I remember that when my mother was ailing she told me again and again that she needed to confess something to me, that there was something I had to know. She said she needed to explain to me the reason why I was a miracle. I always responded, "Mama, there is nothing I need to hear about the past, don't worry, tell me another day." She always repeated these words, "One day Little Mynor, one day you will know the truth. Maybe I will tell you myself. Otherwise, the day will come when you will know and you will remember that today I told you: You are a miracle." I also remember other similar expressions like, "Oh Little Mynor, if I tell you everything, you would realize that you are a pure miracle of God." In reality I never suspected that my beloved mother had at one point made the decision to interrupt my birth; that is almost inconceivable. But now I understand perfectly the reason for the big secret: Extreme poverty and not having a personal relationship with the Lord Jesus Christ, because of that and only that, the greatest woman I have ever known almost allowed her youngest son to die. I do not want to leave out one important fact. Many times my mother looked at me intently and said,

"Who would have thought that you would grow up to be

such a great man, son? Little Mynor, only in the plans and mind of God could something like that exist..."

I didn't understand all the meaning behind her words. I asked her very little in respect to them, and never got to the bottom of the subject. In the middle of these kinds of conversations, she also said to my sister Magda:

"Look Magda, look at what a beautiful son Little Mynor is, who would have thought, right Madga?"

On other opportunities, always speaking of my older sister, my mother contemplated me and said:

"Look Magda, what a great son God gave me."

There is another scene in my memory as well. Every time I took my mother to the emergency room in the hospital, passing the nights without sleep while taking care of her, she said,

"Son, it's a good thing God saved your life."

Each time she said that, I thought she was referring to the time when she was choking on the pill stuck in her throat, or when I was saved during the tropical storm. Even then when I heard over and over again these kinds of comments, it was far from my imagination to think that there was a secret being kept. The times my mother wanted to confess, I stopped her, I don't know why, but that's how it happened.

My mother is with the Lord now, but to the memory of her and in her honor I say, "Mama, there is nothing to forgive you for, you always loved me and were the best mother in the world. If it is necessary to forgive you for what you never did, I forgive you with all my heart. Remember that God preserved my life in your womb, that womb you lent me for nine months. Remember also how much you loved me and spoiled me from the time I was born until your last breath, for 44 years of my life you only knew how to love me, love me, and continue loving me. I love you mother, I'll see you in heaven" (R.I.P.).

2

MIRACLES IN
MY CHILDHOOD

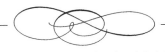

"The head of the family consulted with his wife and made the decision once and for all. They could not continue living on that remote mountain. The situation was unbearable. You could almost touch the poverty with your hands. Life was not life anymore. So they took their five children, their few belongings and moved to Llano Verde, Rio Hondo, Zacapa, the place of origin of the head of that home. There they lived for two years, but the living conditions were not much better. To top it all off the military and the guerrillas were constantly coming into the village and setting up temporary camps there. Carlos and Salvador, two of their sons were now youth and could be recruited by either of the two bands. It was no longer convenient to continue living there. They felt like they were being rained on when they were already wet, or that the sky was closing in on the earth and there was no more room for them. So once again they found it necessary to search for new horizons. They took their few belongings (and as you already know), their five children and headed toward the capital city of Guatemala, running from the poverty and civil war. They did not take many things, but they did carry a lot of faith and hope. They moved into a small room in zone 4 in the city, where they lived only two months. In that place there was no clean drinking water, and so they had to carry water in buckets. When they arrived at the house with water, they would be sweating and fatigued because they had to carry the water a distance of four blocks, or four hundred meters. There was a thief committing crimes all over the neighborhood, but he never robbed the parent's room. To add to that, the mother lent him their new and famous Philips radio transmitter (it was the most precious jewel in their family), and the thief never stole it. He always brought it back, punctually and intact, after listening to a soccer game. After living for two months in that place, they moved to a bigger room in zone 8, where approximately ten other families lived in extreme poverty. They lived there for four months. The head of the family applied for a job at Aldana Brothers and Company, Ltd. There he worked for many years, earning the trust of the owners. During that time, the family moved back to a property in zone 4 because they were the caretakers. Little by little, God made them prosper."

The story I just shared, forms part of my childhood. I was two years old when my parents moved to Llano Verde and four when they moved to the capital of Guatemala. As you know, Guatemala experienced a bloody civil war for 36 long years which took more than 200,000 lives, the majority being unarmed indigenous people. My family sought a place to take refuge from the massacres that were performed by the leftist guerrillas. Death squads of the right wing military and paramilitary in the country killed just as much. The massacres, kidnappings and torture of non-combatants, as well as every other kind of violation of human rights, was our daily bread. My parents took refuge from the war in the capital city with the hope of getting out of poverty as well. Thanks be to God, both things were achieved, even though several years passed before they could offer us a better lifestyle.

Childhood is the period of life that extends from birth until adolescence. It is the time when one is defenseless, a time when one learns to walk, talk and use senses. It is the time when character is formed; principles and values that a person possesses in their adult life. Childhood is a beautiful time when it is not warped by someone or something. It is the time of innocence and purity, to learn, laugh and play. I had the blessing of being part of a close family. We were poor, but totally united, and they taught me moral values. That allowed me to live a normal childhood. My toys were simple: Lids or metal caps from soda bottles which I used as, among other ways, wheels for my cars, made from pieces of wood and morros (a big, inedible fruit, from a tree that grows in Guatemala), and a dreidel, a spinning top. That ends my list of toys. However, I was happy with them.

I can see during my childhood two gigantic miracles worked by the hand of God. Every miracle that happens has a purpose, for that reason I try to understand what the purpose is for each miracle. I see clearly that God preserved my life on many occasions with the one purpose: That I might serve him for special assignments. Dr. Mike Murdock explained it that way and backed it up with a wide range of Bible verses, which give reason to his philosophy on the Christian life. If we as humans do everything with a specific end in mind, wouldn't our wonderful God do the same thing? That is why I am convinced that each miracle that God has done in my life was a special design. Therefore, let's not wait any longer and learn about these two miracles in my infancy.

UNDER THE WHEELS OF A JEEP

Four and a half decades have passed and I don't remember ever telling this story to anyone. But enough with the silence! Today I will bare my life and you are my witness. When I was just seven years old we lived on a car lot called "Super Autos Jack" located on 6a Avenue 8-08 Zone 4. We got there by a miracle of God. My parents as you already know were running because of poverty, first from the mountains and later from their own village. They arrived at a place which they shared with more or less 10 families in extreme poverty; that was in zone 8 of the capital city. My father (Papa Cundo) found a job at which he rose almost immediately to Chief of Staff and later General Manager of Aldana Brothers and Company Limited. It was there, while in Aldana Brothers Company that a Gringo (North American) called Mister Jack arrived, looking for a "guard" to care of his cars at night. My father was selected as the man who was most trustworthy. That caused us to move onto the lot of "Super Autos Jack" for five years. My father watched during the night and the whole family, now eight people, were living in two rooms built from wood.

How did I end up under the wheels of a jeep? Let's see. I'll explain it this way. I was seven years old and I used to play with two children across the street, they were from the middle class and we were from the lowest class. Let me clarify that I do not classify people, but sadly in my country they do. One of those children was Edwin and the other had curly blond hair. This child was the son of rich parents and had a lot of electronic and beautiful toys. He lived the dream of every child who wanted to have lots of toys. One morning I went over to Edwin's house, to invite him to the "Goldilocks" kid's house. Since I couldn't find Edwin, I decided to go alone to the goldilocks kid's house.

I didn't find anyone there either. I insisted, ringing the bell once, twice, three times and many more, but obviously nobody wanted to open the door to the snotty, filthy child in tattered clothes. So I turned around and returned to the property.

For some reason, not finding anyone to play with, I started spinning in circles and circles as I tried to run forward. My little game was not the greatest, because a soon as I would stop, I would start all over again, trying to run at the same time (wow, what a game, boy!). That caused me to lose my orientation and step out of the sidewalk, off the curb, and then without even realizing it I found myself in the middle of the street. Soon, I saw a beige colored Jeep coming full speed towards me. The driver (who I want God to bless so much), did all he could to miss me. He swerved out of his lane to the other side until he hit the curb. It was very quick and effective handiwork in an effort not to kill me. During all of that, I continued spinning. I finally lost all notion of where I was and fell to the ground slightly scraping my elbows and totally losing consciousness for a few brief seconds. When I opened my eyes, there was a big surprise: I saw thick black tires in front of my face. They belonged to the Jeep which managed to brake just before running me over. Otherwise, it would have run over my head. I do not exaggerate in saying that one millisecond more and that Jeep would have torn my head apart, killing me instantaneously. The driver screamed desperately because of all the commotion, thinking he had killed me. His wife and children inside the car also screamed scandalously because I was beneath the Jeep. What do you think happened? All of a sudden, like some kind of Hollywood movie with special effects, I emerged from below the Jeep safe and sound...

The entire family was pale and surprised. It looked as if they had seen a ghost. For several seconds they sat there without speaking or moving. They didn't take their eyes off the little boy with his short sleeve shirt who was rubbing his scraped elbows. After a moment the driver screamed at me, "IDIOOOOOOOOT!" That was only the beginning (ha, ha, ha, ha). Later the woman called me, "Mule headed boy" and the whole family continued screaming at me and insulting me. As soon as I could, I ran full speed away from them until they lost sight of me. To this day, they don't know how close they came to killing a preacher known around the world (ha, ha, ha, ha). Forgive me my dear reader, but as I write this I am dying of laughter (that's just a saying, but I do it as I realize that I really am "hard to kill"). Thank God that Jeep wasn't able to do it. The Lord made that driver stop just before squashing me. Yes, I realize that I was in a total predicament but also that it was a total miracle!

A LETHAL INJECTION

Let's move on to the second miracle during my childhood. My mother, "Mama Mina", always worried because I would never gain weight. So, I was always a sickly weakling (that is what they call skinny children in Guatemala). She gave me a lot of food, but I had my ways of getting rid of it. What really happened was that when Mama Mina looked somewhere else, I would take the chicken legs, the tortillas, and whatever other food and pass it to my little friend Edwin Bolanos. You may not believe it, but to this day I am thin and my friend Bolanos is chubby.

I was eight years old when my mother took me to the public clinic of zone 4 at the bus terminal. I explain with so much detail so that you know, and understand that my beloved mother did not take me to a private clinic or hospital, but something almost equal to a slaughterhouse. Poverty forced us to find the cheapest, or free medical attention.

"My son is lethargic, look how thin he is," my mother said to the supposed doctor.

She replied, "Maybe he is sick.

We will give him some anti-worm medicine in case he has parasites, and I will prescribe some McCoy vitamins made from Cod liver extract for him as well. Also, just in case there is some kind of infection, WE WILL INJECT HIM WITH PENECILLIN," she said.

Perhaps it was in ignorance, my mother's and the doctor's or nurses', that they did not know that before giving this potent antibiotic called Penicillin, a specific analysis should be done to determine if the patient is allergic or not. It is true that for a long time, it was thought unnecessary to do a study before administering it to patients, because allergic reactions were not frequent. After making a diagnosis by plain sight, without any kind of tests, that woman proceeded to administer a gigantic injection of penicillin, and to top it all off, I am **deathly allergic.**

She hadn't even finished administering said dose when the fluid was already affecting me. I started to feel some strong reactions… I fell to the floor repeatedly, and I had difficulty breathing. My mother was worried, and in her ignorance said, "Doctor, let me take him home how he is, in the house I'll give him some broth and revive him."

The doctor seemed to wake up and realized the gravity of the situation. Being very nervous, she shouted at my mother, "Lady, Lady, you don't know what's happening. Your son is dying and if you take him how he is now, he will not make it to the house alive."

My mother didn't say a word, she was speechless from fright. The doctor continued, saying, "Look, fortunately we have shots against penicillin and we will inject him as many times as it takes to revive your little boy...."

I remember the words of that doctor as if she said it today, pleading my mother not to take me and to realize the gravity of the situation. My sister Trinis was there and she confirms everything that happened. Glory to God for that doctor, because even though in one moment she almost killed me, in the next she became my guardian angel (God was there in all of this, He always cared for me)! The story is long, but it ends with this: we went through an entire day, morning and afternoon in the dirty, foul smelling clinic for people in extreme poverty. They gave me a total of 14 injections (shots). That day I ended up having needles in every part of my buttocks, but once again I CAME OUT ALIVE! Hallelujah, Glory to God!
The story of my near death because of Penicillin is over, but my thankfulness to God continues strong. My beloved reader, I know of these and other things that occurred in my life, and I remember a considerable part. My family has told me the remaining details. I ask myself, how many other times has God saved me that I don't know about, and how many times has God saved you?...

God is not just my God, he is yours as well. He is "our Father who is in heaven and every other place." I do not have any special privileges. He loves us all the same. I do not doubt that your life could also be written in a book, and be equally or even more exciting than mine. There are so many untold miracles, like unprocessed gold. David the psalmist said: *"Open thou mine eyes, that I may behold wondrous things out of thy law"* (Psalm 119:18). Many times we want to see the latest Mercedes Benz parked in front of our "mansion" to be able to testify that God does miracles, but the truth is that God cannot be dollarized. Rich or poor, God is close to you to free you, to heal you, to care for you and do you good. I invite you to take some free time and sanctify Him. Take a moment alone and give thanks to God for all his wonders and all his blessings and favors poured out onto your life. Do it soon, do it today, do it right now, amen.

WE CAME OUT OF POVERTY TO LOVE AND HELP THE POOR

I cannot finish this chapter without mentioning an important detail. I have emphasized that my family comes from extreme poverty. However, God took us out of that poverty. Hard work, taking advantage of opportunities, strength, desire to get ahead and perseverance were the factors that God used so that we could accomplish it. However, we never forgot the poor. On the contrary, my mother left us an example. Without any legal adoption papers, my mother adopted two children whose mother could not sustain them. They also adopted "Mama Mina" in their hearts and I also see them as two adopted brothers. Despite us being a numerous family, God worked a miracle and provided enough for two more mouths to feed and clothe, buy shoes for, and give the basics to Daniel and Apolo Mendez. Daniel arrived when he was 9 years old and left when he was a young man. Later, Apolo arrived at a similar age until he was an older youth. Also, for many years my mother bought bread every day for several families with low resources and did many good works.

Knowing poverty taught us to love the poor. My brother
Carlos Vargas is the Founder and Director of a Charity
Ministry of an international level called "Hope of Life"
(for more information visit the web site www.esvida.
org). Currently, this ministry has an elderly home where
approximately 65 elderly people live, an orphanage which
houses approximately 150 orphan children, a Christian
School where more than 300 students are learning, and,
among other projects, a Nutritional Center where more
than 50 malnourished children at a time recuperate. Also,
he is building a Children's Hospital where quality medical
attention will be given with adequate treatment and
medicine without cost. In the majority of the cases, the
medical attention and treatment will be totally free. There
will only be certain cases where they will charge someone;
that being if the person is capable of paying. The initial
cost of this Hospital exceeds 7 million dollars. The goal
is to be able to save the lives of children with problems
of malnutrition and transform that of those with certain
physical limitations. They will also attend to pregnant
women, administer birth control and educate regarding
prenatal prevention; in this way reducing maternal and
child mortality.

My brother Salvador, for his part, since he founded Shalom
Christian Temple 29 years ago, gave away the first offering
he collected in the first month, which was $787.00. He
did the same thing the second month with $1,280.00 and
$1,800.00 the third. In the same way he donated the fourth,
and the fifth, and in that way successively gave away all
the offerings and tithes for many years. My sisters Trinis,
Magda and Lety are always providing for some child in
need. I still remember that together with my mother and
father they took up monthly collections within themselves
to send what was collected to poor families and helpless
children.

On my part, although I have not done such great works in social areas, I am characterized more for continuously helping homeless people. Together with my adopted brother Daniel Mendez, we walked the streets of Guatemala giving away 0.25 quetzal cent coins and bills of one and five quetzals. The place that I was fascinated to walk through was from 6th avenue to 10th street until the famous 18th street in zone 1. I did that almost every week for a year and a half. My pilgrimage was giving away the famous Guatemalan "Chocas" (known as Quarters in the United States). At the end of 6th avenue I found a lot of beggars and I would give money to each one of them. Today I continue doing so. Almost every day vagrants and wanderers will arrive at my house to ask me for money. Not only do I give them my money, but I give them food and my clothes fresh from the drycleaner's. Almost all of the homeless people in the neighborhood are my friends and seek me out every day. I have presented Jesus as Savior to all of them. In Shalom Christian Temple, every Saturday and Sunday I have the wandering and needy who listen to the message and at the end wait for me to give them money to eat. What a true pleasure it is for me to do that as a lifestyle! For Christmas, Thanksgiving, for their birthdays and other holidays I am the only one who gives them gifts. As I write this part of my autobiography, I just celebrated the birthday of Josepho, a homeless man who was blind and for who we arranged a surgery and now he can see. The party was beautiful; he and I were dressed in matching black suits. We had the same jacket, the same brand, the same color; the same shirt and tie. We looked like twins. The only small difference was that he is a tall African American and I am a Latino of medium stature. All of this is my pleasure and the delight of my life.

As I write, my lawyers and I are in the arrangements of my new corporation, "Shalom Philanthropy", it is my own foundation created to promote "A Better Life." And so, of poverty I have nothing more than the memory. Although I am not swimming in money, I am also not drowning in scarcity. Hallelujah, Glory to God!

3

THE BIGGEST MIRACLE

"They were 30 consecutive days of evangelistic campaigns in the popular "La Florida Colony", Zone 19 of the capital city of Guatemala. The tent that was used to celebrate had a capacity of 2,000 people and was set up in front of the municipal market. Night after night it filled with humble and thirsty people. The preachers were missionary siblings Glen and Charlet from the United States. The benches were made from three blocks of cement for legs, and a rustic board of one inch thick wood, it was 10 inches wide and 12 feet long. The dirt floor was adorned with sawdust. From the roof hung common light bulbs that illuminated the grand grey tent which had the appearance of one from the circus. An hour before the meetings would start, someone played the organ and sang a beloved and preferred hymn which had the words, "Savior, great doctor, my Christ Jesus, oh hallelujah, glory be to him." That song would be repeated over and over again. There was a 9 year old boy present during several of those glorious nights, accompanied by his mother and a domestic servant. In the days before, many people had given their lives to Christ, including the domestic servant. The time had arrived to preach and the boy was very attentive to each word he heard. The sermon was challenging and at the end of it, an evangelistic invitation was given and the little one asked:

"Mama, can I go forward and accept Jesus?"

"Of course dear little son," responded the woman. "Chon (the servant) will accompany you," she added.

"No," said the daring boy, "I will go alone."

That unforgettable story happened 37 years ago. That is to say, in the year 1973, and that daring boy who made Jesus the savior of his soul, was me. Although I was born in the cradle of a family that feared God and was raised in a house that respected the Gospel, I personally felt a profound call from Jesus to my heart. I answered his call and my life has never been the same. Since the day I was saved I have never feared losing my salvation, not even for a single second. Jesus called me to save me, not to offer me instructions on how I could save myself through works or through going many times to church, or practicing religion, etc.

This book would not be complete without mentioning "the greatest of all the miracles"; I am referring to the miracle of my salvation. Anyone can be a millionaire or even conquer the whole earth, but if he loses his soul, all the glory in this world will do him no good. *"For what shall it profit a man, if he shall gain the whole world, and lose his own soul?"* (Mark 8:36). For everything a human being can manage to accumulate, when he dies he can't take any of it with him, it all stays here. The only eternal thing is the soul, and the only way to save it from eternal condemnation is through the redemptive work of Jesus Christ.

My decision was firm! The preacher was focused on a

middle aged audience, on humble and hardworking people, but to the surprise of all, there was a 9 year old boy giving absolute attention and during the call from the altar, he was one of the first to pass forward. Since then the devil has wanted to put a stop to my party. Satan is a liar, the father of lies and he wanted to discourage me. When the multitude went forward, they prayed for those who made Jesus the Lord of their lives. They laid hands on them one by one, except on me. The ushers took the names and information of everyone, except mine. I think that nobody valued my decision because I was just a child. Because of that I always take it very seriously when children make a decision for Christ. I constantly take into account what we are told in Matthew 19:14 *"But Jesus said, 'Let the little children come to Me, and do not forbid them; for of such is the kingdom of heaven.'"*

The isolation did not end there. When they gave away copies of the Gospel according to Saint John, they didn't give me anything. Despite the fact that the preacher gave clear instructions to give a brochure of the Gospel according to Saint John to everyone who had made a confession of faith in Christ, when they arrived in front of me, the blundering ushers didn't give me anything because I was a child. The last straw was when they asked everyone who wished to speak with a counselor to stay up front while they sang the last hymn. I obediently stayed there, looking to either side and even though there were sufficient spiritual advisors, nobody came to me to ask about my decision to Christ. For an instant it made me feel like "an invisible boy" (ha, ha, ha, ha). When I returned to my rustic bench where I found my mother seated, she asked me how I felt. I told her that I was fine. It was then that she was able to observe my unforgettable ear to ear smile that betrayed the incomparable joy I felt. I was a new boy and had assurance of salvation. I assure you it was the happiest day of my entire life. Of course I did not understand why they attended everyone else and ignored me. The poor uneducated ushers, didn't know that the boy who was there was a future world travelling preacher. That is the reason why in my crusades, before doing an evangelistic invitation for adults, I always have a children's invitation. My experience has been that hundreds of children have given their lives to Jesus to be saved for the first time. Hallelujah, glory to God for that!

MAINOTAUR CONVERTS

The next day, Chon, the young domestic servant, told someone what happened the night before while in a store in the neighborhood. By that afternoon all my little friends (a gang of children that surpassed some 100 children in the Colony), knew that I had given my life to Jesus. Not everyone understood what that meant, but they interrogated me about it. Some of them made fun of me while others admired me for my boldness. I remember my dear childhood friend "El Chiqui" spread the news saying, "Mainotaur (that is what my friends called me at the time), is an Evangelical Muchá" (a Guatemalan expression, or saying which can refer to a guy or a girl). El Chiqui finalized the expression by saying, "Can you believe it? Mainotaur is an evangelical now." However, when alone, Chiqui called me and asked me about Jesus, heaven, the stars, the planets and beyond, and about eternal life… Who would have imagined that children of such a young age would already be asking about that, and talking amongst themselves in respect to it? In my adult years I have had the privilege of leading my friend "El Chiqui" to Jesus, and have also led many more of my childhood friends as well. I introduced them to Jesus so he would save them. How good it is that Jesus is not religious, he doesn't place conditions; the Bible says: *"Believe on the Lord Jesus Christ, and thou shalt be saved, and thy house"* (Acts 16:31).

Many believe that in order to be saved one must call himself Evangelical, others are called Baptists, Methodists, Pentecostals, Presbyterians, Lutherans, etc. None of these churches are bad, the bad is in believing that one church or religion offers salvation. The only one who saves is named Jesus of Nazareth. That is why in my sermons I invite my audience to have a relationship with Jesus Christ, I don't teach a religion.

After nearly 30 years of ministry, I have seen every kind of miracle, including watching people brought back from the brink of death. People considered hopeless by doctors and only lying in wait for their last breath. I've seen them come back to life. I have also been the witness of healings of cancer, miracles of protection from threats against life, miracles of financial provision, etc., etc., but no miracle as great as the salvation of my soul. When Jesus saved me, he gave me the right to be a child of God. *"But as many as received him, to them gave he power to become the sons of God, even to them that believe on his name."* (John 1:12). He gave me the privilege of being the heir of the Father, and the joint-heir with the Son. *"And if children, then heirs; heirs of God, and joint-heirs with Christ; if so be that we suffer with him, that we may be also glorified together."* (Romans 8:17). He gave me the blessing of being the Temple of the Holy Spirit. *"What? Know ye not that your body is the temple of the Holy Ghost which is in you, which ye have of God, and ye are not your own?"* (1 Corinthians 6:19). What more can I expect but eternal life with the saved, together with the Father, the Son and the Holy Spirit. Amen.

The biggest miracle in my life is not waiting to happen, it already did. Christ is not going to save me, he has already saved me! The miracle begins here on planet earth. My life is free of vices, of bad works and of dangers. As a saved person, I produce fruits worthy of repentance. I am a man faithful to my wife, faithful to my children, faithful to my friends, faithful to the call and faithful to God. With this I do not pretend to indicate that I am perfect. I would be a liar in saying that I have not sinned, I have. I have committed sins small, medium and even big if you wanted to classify them in that way. The difference is that I am a repented sinner, and little by little God makes my steps firmer and I am growing progressively. *"But the path of the just is as the shining light, that shineth more and more unto the perfect day"* (Proverbs 4:18).

If I had not met Jesus and did not have an intimate relationship with him, I could not be sure that my home would be functional; I doubt that my children would be okay. Also, I'm not sure if I would be alive since I am so energetic, and surely my boldness would have taken me down some bad roads. Giving myself to Christ from the time I was a child was the best thing I could have done. Some people in their ignorance tell me that I did not enjoy life, because I became evangelical very young. I think that they do not know even the littlest bit of what it means to "enjoy life." I am a man who is completely happy, satisfied, and I wake up each morning full of encouragement and with a great expectation of what God is going to do that day in my favor.

I BRIEFLY LEFT THE PATH

I have emphasized that I am not perfect, and it would be absurd to try and insinuate it because nobody would believe me. When I was 13 years old I separated from close communion with Jesus, although I am convinced that I never lost my salvation. Christ saved me from the time I surrendered my life to Him. I stopped going to church and I joined with some friends who exercised a negative influence in my life. Like the prodigal son, I was far from home, doing what I wanted and wasting the privileges of a child of God. I learned to smoke. It never became an addiction but I did smoke. Thank God I only practiced it as a passing habit. I remember that the more bad habits I practiced, the more temptations my friends would bring. They got me to smoke marijuana. I probably only smoked a total of three tiny, ultra-thin cigarettes, but I did try marijuana. The week I tried to renew my vows to the Lord, they brought me LSD pills (similar to XTC or Ecstasy); my decision to rededicate my life to Christ and reconcile was so strong that I never again practiced those things. Other sins that are not worth mentioning were in my daily life, but I don't think it would bless anyone to confess the things the devil made me take or do. However, I leave it clear that I have sinned, and today I am a repented person. Because of that, I believe it is worth it to delve into what Christ did in me, and not in what the devil induced me to do. The day I met Him and the day I reconciled, He gave me of His water and I have never been thirsty again; but He came to be a fountain in me, from which unquenchable eternal life springs.

I was 14 years and 9 months old when my brother Salvador was initiating the church in Providence, Rhode Island. I was taken to the services almost by force. I did not want to pay any attention, but I did it to show a certain respect. At the moment of the call or invitation, the words were cutting, like a double-edged sword. Salvador said, "The train of life is leaving, the brothers who are on the roll call list and those who give their lives to Christ today will have their names written in the book of life"... He repeated this several times. As he said it, I knew that it wasn't my brother Salvador, but it was Jesus Himself who saved me when I was 9 years old, and who was calling me into a direct and close relationship with Him, to later prepare me in my call to Priesthood. Since I was a child I never saw myself as just another evangelical, I imagined myself like a Yiye Avila or a Billy Graham (what a pretentious thought...).

RENEWING MY DECISION FOR JESUS

I remember perfectly the 27th of April in the year 1980. I couldn't take it anymore, and without thinking I made my way up to the front. The altar was in the living room of my parent's house, that was where they celebrated their services and that was where I decided once and for all to harmonize my life with the Savior of the world. My brother Salvador who was the Pastor, together with the other brothers, prayed for me. My transformation was not very credible at all. In those days I had met the love of my life. Her name was Blanqui. Everyone thought that I had made new vows to God because if I didn't, her parents wouldn't let me be her boyfriend... The truth was that I did it because my soul was thirsty for God, the living God. I couldn't sleep during the nights, thinking, "When shall I come and appear before God? My tears have been my bread day and night" (Psalm 42:2, 3).

THE WORST NIGHTMARE

The night before the event I just described, I had a horrible dream where I was dying, drowning in a pool. After ending up face down at the bottom of it, I could see (in the dream) how my soul descended into hell. There, a very nice person said to me, "Hello friend." When I came near with confidence to greet the very good looking person, he immediately took of his mask of cordiality and I saw what I understood to be the face of the devil. He laughed at me and roared, saying, "YOU WERE WRONG, you will spend eternity here, ha, ha, ha, ha." Before such an impacting picture, I screamed very loud begging for help from my Savior, to Jesus who at age 9 saved me. This dream was so terrifying that I have called it "The Worst Nightmare." I screamed so loud that Mama Mina and Papa Cundo came to my room to see what was happening to me. The dream had been so real that my scream was heard throughout the whole house. I said, "Jesus, Jesus, don't leave me here, forgive me and if you take me out, I will give my whole life to your service. I just ask for one more opportunity. Take me out Jesus, forgive me, and free me." When my parents arrived and woke me up, I told them, so as to not worry them, that everything was fine and that I just had a nightmare. That night I couldn't sleep, I was sweating like I never had before in my life. I felt like I had just come out of hell itself even though the dream was over. The next day there was a service in my house. My brother Salvador gave the call that I mentioned earlier and from that holy day, my life changed only for good. Today I serve God; I do it because I am thankful toward him and also to help many others to be saved through Jesus Christ. The interesting thing is that each time I have felt weak, Jesus has helped me. When I have sinned, Jesus has not condemned me, instead he has advocated for me. Who could find a better intercessor and Savior? NOBODY! Knowing Jesus is the best thing that can happen in the life of any human, because of that I never tire of inviting my listeners to have a personal encounter with him.

ARE YOU SAVED?

Due to the fact that you are reading my autobiography, you know quite a lot about me. However, my dear reader, I don't know who you are. What I do know is that we all need to be saved from eternal condemnation. The Bible says, *"For all have sinned, and come short of the glory of God"* (Romans 3:23). It also says, *"And as it is appointed unto men once to die, but after this the judgment"* (Hebrews 9:27). It is for that reason I ask you: Are you saved? There is only one way to be so, that is recognizing the work of Christ Jesus on the cross of Calvary, taking your place in order to offer you eternal salvation. The only thing you must do to be saved is come repented before him and recognize him as your absolute Redeemer and Lord.

It is not about forming part of a specific church or having a religion. Churches, religions and denominations cannot offer salvation for your soul. Since the time our first parents Adam and Eve failed God, sin entered the world and extended to all humanity. However, God had a plan of redemption which is immediately mentioned in Genesis 3:15. Now you and I, we don't have to make sacrifices or burnt offerings. All that is necessary is going to Jesus for him to save us.

Friend, if you have never permitted Christ to be the master of your life and have never recognized him as your personal Savior, why don't you do it today? If you have done it before, but you find yourself far from your beloved Father, why not come back today and restore that relationship with him. *"Behold, now is the accepted time; behold, now is the day of salvation"* says God (2 Corinthians 6:2). In another place, Jesus expressed in his own words, *"Behold, I stand at the door, and knock: if any man hear my voice, and open the door, I will come in to him, and will sup with him, and he with me"* (Revelation 3:20). No doubt that a possible reason why God permitted you to read this book, is so that you will come back to Jesus, to renew your relationship with him. If you already serve him and live in communion with him, why not take advantage of and pray the last prayer that is suggested in this chapter? It is the prayer of the servant who is willing to be faithful with his gift or talent. My dear reader, you are not reading "A Life of Miracles" by mere chance, this is part of the plan of God for your life. There is a call to answer. Do it today by repeating one of the following three prayers with me. Do not leave it for another day, do it today.

THE SINNER'S PRAYER

"Lord Jesus, I recognize that I am a sinner and that without you I am not saved, and eternal condemnation awaits me. Today I come repentant of my sins. I ask you to save me, and that you wash away every stain of sin that exists in my life with your precious blood, and let my name be written in the book of life. I accept you as my Lord and sufficient Savior. I pray this in the name of Jesus, amen.

THE PRAYER OF VOW RENEWAL

"Lord Jesus, I know the day I accepted you; you saved me and protected my soul. I know that nobody can snatch me from your hand. However, I recognize that I have been a disobedient son, and I find myself far from home like the prodigal son. Today I ask you for forgiveness. I ask you to revive the joy of my salvation and help me to give fruits worthy of repentance and to maintain a close relationship with you, going to church each week. Thank you because all this time I have been far away, you have not left me for even an instant. You did not condemn me; you were just waiting for my return home. Thank you for embracing me and receiving me as your son. I lift up this sincere and deep prayer in the name of Jesus, amen.

PRAYER OF THE FAITHFUL SERVANT

"Lord Jesus, in Reading this blessed book, I realize that even though I am already saved and I have not been far from you, with all of that, I recognize that I have not been faithful in my service. I have discovered that I have not used faithfully the gifts and talents that you have given me for the edification of others. I have not been a witness of your salvation and my light has not shined on others for them to be saved. Forgive me and help me to serve you from now on. So that, in addition to congregating, singing, listening to sermons, faithfully giving offerings and tithes, I can be a useful instrument in your hands. Let me be in the midst of a lost world, a light to those who live in darkness. God, today I surrender my life to your service, to win many through the message of salvation by faith and grace. I pray this in the name of Jesus, amen.

4

MIRACLES
IN THE AIR

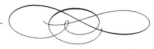

"They were three long weeks, 21 long days of combat, 504 hours to be exact, the equivalent of 30,240 minutes. During all this time a fierce battle was waged. The demonic principalities of Persia and Greece tried to impede Michael the archangel and another group of God's angels, as they carried to Daniel the answer to his prayers. The servant of God had received a vision, but he didn't understand it, so he asked God to show him the meaning (Daniel 10:1-14). The angel visited Daniel, and informed him that his prayers had been heard from the moment he said them and they had left the general headquarters of the angels to bring him the answer, but on the road they found evil spirits of high rank who fought to stop that answer from being delivered. That is to say, the forces of evil against the army of God waged a fierce battle in the air."

As you have already realized, the above is a Bible story that shows us the reality of what many times goes on above us. While we live here on earth, in the heavens there is a spiritual war being waged. In Ephesians 6:12 Paul explains it in this way: *"For we wrestle not against flesh and blood, but against principalities, against powers, against the rulers of the darkness of this world, against spiritual wickedness in high places."*

Here it speaks of *"principalities"* or evil spirits who are responsible for a specific territory; the text in Daniel is an example of that. It also mentions *"powers and rulers"*, or fallen angels who have dominion over a jurisdiction. Finally, it mentions *"spiritual wickedness"*, or demons who are dedicated to block or try to obstruct the work of Christ and the workers of Christ. In 1 Thessalonians 2:18 Paul explains to the Christians of that region: *"Wherefore we would have come unto you, even I Paul, once and again; but Satan hindered us."* That means that Satan stopped them.

As a Servant of God, I am conscious that the enemy of our souls and his spiritual forces are fighting in the heavens to stop us from advancing the work of God, including ending our own lives. I understand that God has worked in my life several miracles in the air, it is for that reason I present the subject in this chapter.

Being that I live a good part of my life in the air due to the fact that I have travelled more than two million miles on American Airlines alone, it has been the place of many miracles. My travels are so frequent, that during this month while I write this chapter (June of 2010), I have slept four nights in four different planes. Generally I prefer to travel at night, so I can arrive home in the morning and share with my family; that way I gain one more day.

MY FIRST INTERSTATE TRIP

I was only 19 years old when I made my first interstate ministry trip, or outside of the State where I lived, within the United States of North America. My schedule consisted of a twenty-one day tour through four different cities in three states. It was set up in the following way: Seven days in Chicago, Illinois; seven days in Los Angeles, California and seven days between Midland and Odessa, Texas. At that time I had the joy and privilege of having a coordinator. His name was Reverend Herlindo Morales, who dared to promote me at such a young age.

Herlindo heard me talk about my desire to travel and preach in Evangelistic Crusades. While we spoke about the subject on one occasion he asked me, "And when are you planning on diving in?"

I responded, "When I find a coordinator."

"You already have one," was his reply. "Today I will start preparing a schedule for you," he added.

In less than ten days not only did we have a full schedule, but all the tickets were bought and a scandal came up among my acquaintances. The opinions were diverse: Some were joyful; others did not believe it and others criticized me. There were some who said I was doing it to show off and not for "ministry." Now that I remember it, the situation makes me laugh. Being a youth of just 19 years and I was already experiencing the privilege of being criticized (ha, ha, ha, ha,).

AN EXTRA DOLLAR

The price of the tickets was the first miracle of my first ministerial trip. I only had $400.00 available, NO MORE! Herlindo said to me: "Don't you worry, you pay for your ticket and I'll pay for mine." I called Intercontinental Travel, owned by my friend Vladimir Rodriguez. I told Ramon, the travel agent, to find me the most economic tickets possible for the whole tour. I explained to him that

I was an evangelist and I had no money. Ramon took it with a laugh, but at the same time very seriously. Within an hour he had the tickets reserved and ready for payment. Without knowing how much money I had available, he told me, "The cheapest I could find is $399.00 per person, for the entire tour." I simply could not believe it! I had $400.00, so that left me with one extra dollar for the rest of the tour. I did not doubt it for even an instant, this was my first evangelistic tour through four cities and my coordinator would pay for his tickets, what more could I ask for? I immediately confirmed the trip and proceeded to pay for the tickets.

WE FELT LIKE OWNERS

We went into the US Airways airplane with zero flight experience, we knew nothing about it. But there we were, my coordinator Reverend Morales and I, the young preacher. We left for Shiloh Church which was pastored by my great friend and soul brother, Dr. Roberto Ramazzini.

As soon as Herlindo sat down, he started asking for beverages. The plane hadn't even started toward the runway; it hadn't even shut the doors when he pressed the button for the airline attendant. She arrived to ask what the emergency was and he, with lots of style, said, "Coca Cola please." The airline attendant could have told him that it was not a restaurant and that drinks would be served when the plane reached navigation altitude, but she preferred to be cordial and went to get it. When she brought it, Herlindo said to her, "Two Coca Colas, please," one was for him and the other for me. I thought they were going to kick us off the plane, but since the girl saw that we had novice faces, she went to bring the second Coca Cola. At that time I knew nothing about flying in First Class; I didn't even know how to fly in economy class. More than that, we didn't even know anything about how to act on an airplane. The only thing I remember is that we felt like the owners of US Airways.

I brought a carrier bag totally filled with suits. In it were 26 ties of every kind of color. I remember the amount because one little boy saw them, and told his mother that he never thought anyone could have so many. I also carried a giant suitcase filled with other kinds of clothes. Aside from that, I brought my brown leather briefcase, my Canon AE1 photo camera and a Panasonic VHS video camera. That was advanced technology in those days. There was also another silver, metal suitcase where we carried Cinematographic lights. I think that from a young age I already had style, at least my own style (God forgive me for all these assumptions…ha, ha, ha, ha). In my mind, I was thinking in greatness and excellence. That was the first time I left my city to preach outside. It was all smooth sailing. My fiery coordinator was travelling with me and offered to take action in an instant if I forgot the messages. He would come and finish the sermon, and he would do it in a natural way that would seem as if we planned it. There was nothing else I could have wanted.

SMOKE CAME OUT OF THE TURBINE

Up until then everything had been going perfectly fine and our joy was immense. But since my very first ministerial journey the devil started his attacks against my person and ministry. Unexpectedly, smoke started coming out one side of the plane. I was the one who discovered it. As I was looking out the window I saw that a lot of smoke was coming out of the right turbine. We were at the point of arriving in Chicago, when a stream of soot could be seen marking the sky, all of it coming from the turbine. I quickly pressed the button to call the airline attendant. She arrived with a long face believing that I wanted another Coca Cola, and she asked me what she could serve me. I just whispered, "Look" and pointed. That was when I discovered that she too was a novice and went to call the person in charge. That person also did not know what to do and passed on the message to the cabin. Seconds later, the captain himself came out and looked out my window to see the stream of smoke flowing out of the turbine. I think that if something like that happens today, all the television channels would show it live. Well, at that time not even CNN existed, it was founded in 1980 by Ted Turner.

I will finish the story by telling you that the smoke continued coming out, and more with each moment. Later, the airplane began to shake violently, like when they go through turbulence. They put us on alert and almost everyone was filled with panic. I say almost everyone, because Herlindo and I felt NO fear. Our faith was as pure as that of a child. It never passed through our minds that we might die in the air, because we were on a Christian mission. We had to finish what meant to us "the most important evangelistic crusade in our lives" and we knew that the plane would arrive at its destination, and we were in the hands of God. Honestly we seemed like a couple of crazy people who ignored what was happening. We even continued drinking Coca Cola and chatting about ministries, all the while our cups shaking uncontrollably. The plane continued trembling and we acted as if nothing was going on. Such laughter as I remember all of this now! All that remained was for us to ask for more Coca Cola... We simply did not realize that we were on the brink of death. God freed us from it and to him we give the glory and honor, from age to age, amen.

THE THIRD COICOM

I flew a route that from what I understand, no longer exists. It was on American Airlines from Miami to Buenos Aires, Argentina, with a connection through Santiago, Chile. That was where the third COICOM Summit took place. Back then I was already accumulating frequent flyer miles on American and I preferred to fly with several stops while seeking to achieve more frequent flyer miles. In that same way I left from Providence, Rhode Island to JFK in New York. From there I took another flight to Miami, Florida and from Miami I flew to Buenos Aires with a continued connection to Santiago, Chile. The excitement that I felt was the same as my first tour. At that time (although I was financially struggling), I was able to be, for the first time, one of the Official Sponsors of COICOM. Being the sponsor of COICOM during those dates was a complete miracle. My biggest miracle happened when my plane was going to crash. While we were crossing the Andes Mountain Range, we passed through a storm that to this day I consider to be the strongest I have ever experienced. The plane started to tremble, and then shake to such a degree that the food fell out of the trays (during that time they gave food on the planes). The vibrations were stronger and stronger, to the point that the lights on the plane started to flicker. We all had our seat belts on. Some prayed, others did the Sign of the Cross and muttered with their rosaries in their hands, others went pale and many screamed loudly.

A VIOLENT LOSS OF ALTITUDE

It was a serious storm. I think it was a pilot error to risk the storm instead of avoiding it. The panorama could not have been cloudier. After experiencing a couple of small plunges from loss of altitude, there was a moment when, in a violent manner, the planed did not only loose considerable altitude, but also control. It felt like it turned completely on its side as it descended at full speed. The shaking was so strong that one had to grip the seat so that the seat belt wouldn't hurt your abdomen. If one looked outside, one could see flashes, lightning, and all kinds of meteorological phenomenon. If one looked inside, the situation was critical. Never before or after, have I watched someone fly through the air. One man, who did not have his seat belt on correctly, went flying and fell on the legs of another passenger. There was a child, who, from being shaken so much, vomited. I remember seeing the vomit fly as if it was in slow motion as the plane lost altitude and there was little gravity. When the plane recovered and stabilized, the vomit landed on the neck and back of another passenger. The mother tried to say she was sorry, but the passenger told her not to worry about it, that he just wanted to be survive and live. I also observed how giant drops of Coca Cola and wine flew in slow motion. That agony lasted approximately thirty five long minutes of shaking and three minutes of sudden falls.

When the plane finally stabilized on its route, it looked like a market in a poor neighborhood. The floor was covered in lettuce, vegetables, cups of coffee, plates, pieces of chicken, meat, bread, etc. The scene was incredibly difficult to work out, but nobody cared, the only thing we wanted was to land safe and sound. God, who never abandons us, did the miracle; I believe it was out of love, not only for me, but for the other COICOM conference goers who were on that flight. When we arrived to land, there wasn't a person who didn't want to kiss the floor like the Pope and vow "I WILL NEVER GET ON ANOTHER PLANE."

A PLANE WITHOUT FUEL

This is the straw that broke the camel's back. I was in the JFK airport in New York ready to fly to London, Heathrow, to later fly to the Billy Graham event "Amsterdam 2000." There, 10,000 evangelists from all over the planet were meeting, arriving from 190 nations. My desire to go was great; however I also really wanted good seats on the planes. I went to my super luxurious seat in First Class on American Airlines. It was a dream come true for any traveler. Of course, it was not my ultimate dream, what I desired was to fly in a supersonic "Concorde" plane.

I did everything I could to gather together 250,000 miles so I could redeem them for that flight. Anyone who is a frequent traveler would have desired to have the privilege of flying at least one time on the Concorde. That plane could cross the Atlantic in only 3 hours at a speed of 1370 miles per hour, a speed that is double the speed of sound. The speed was so much that the passengers who boarded in Europe could land in New York an hour before they left, because of the time change.

As a professional traveller, I wanted to leave in my life's record that I had been on that blessed flight. However, I did not have the money, since the cost was between $13,000.00 and $15,000.00 per ticket. However with a quarter of a million accumulated miles, British Airways or Delta would allow one to fly on it.

I did everything in my power to earn that amount, which to me was a big challenge. But for all the struggles of consolidating frequent flyer miles from one way to another, and even buying extra miles, I simply did not have enough. I was so close to getting it; all I needed was another 25,000 miles. Therefore, I thought of the possibilities for achieving my objective. I wanted to fly on that plane no matter what. One day, I found myself in front of a computer that I borrowed in my brother Carlos's factory. I started doing a final analysis and investigated ways of mile consolidation to buy the ticket. As I was investigating, on my screen appeared AOL news: "The Concorde falls and crashes close to Charles de Gaulle in Paris; All 113 passengers on board dead." When I read that news, I literally collapsed in the chair and I felt like my legs didn't have the strength to stand. My face went pale and the employee who was passing by asked what was wrong with me. I told him that just then, the plane I wanted to fly on in the next few weeks had crashed. When I mentioned that it was about the famous supersonic Concorde, they made fun of me... something I am used to now. The funny thing is that those who have made fun of my desires in one way or another are the ones who have witnessed me achieving what I propose in the name of Jesus.

So I give thanks to God for two things: First, because I didn't have enough accumulated miles, or a way to consolidate them. Second, because I was not on that flight.

So, I showed up, on what I told you about three paragraphs ago, it was an American Airlines Boeing 777-200, a beautiful and luxurious plane. The attention was presidential or first class. No one could have asked for more. I was going to the biggest event in the history of Christianity in all of humanity. "Amsterdam 2000," with 10,000 evangelists from around the globe and a total cost of thirty-six million dollars. Waiting for me was an ample suite that cost $2,300.00. When the event was over and I went to reception to pay, the receptionist at the hotel told me, "Sir, you don't owe anything; everything has been paid for by the Billy Graham Association." When she told me that, I didn't know if I should take off running before they said it was mistake or just wait. The truth is, I asked again and they confirmed it was true. They said, "THERE IS NO DOUBT, EVERYTHING IS ALREADY PAID FOR. YOU DO NOT OWE ANYTHING." After walking out of the hotel slow and calmly, I bolted at maximum speed disappearing from that luxurious hotel in Holland, Amsterdam called "Golden Tulips."

WHEN DID THE BIGGEST MIRACLE HAPPEN?

The miracles or blessings of this kind were happening to me practically every day; first not flying on the "Concorde." After that, flying from one continent to another First Class without paying a single dollar; it was exchanged for 90,000 frequent flyer miles. Later, the blessing of not having to pay for the luxurious suite. But the biggest act of God, happened, to my understanding, when the pilot realized that the plane, which had already taken off from JFK, New York, toward London, England, did not have any fuel. That fact, just like many other things I described in "A Life of Miracles" could seem unacceptable, illogical, or unbelievable; but they really happened. The plane had taken off and we were about ten minutes into the flight, when the pilot very clearly and honestly explained to us through the speakers: "Surely some of you are going to send our airline the biggest complaint of your lives, but I have to confess to you that this airplane has taken off without any fuel. Ladies and gentlemen: This is incredible, but we are heading to England without a single drop of gasoline." So, the airplane made a 180 degree turn and returned to JFK where they gave us fuel. I personally have written and sent observations of bad service, but this time I did not. The grace of God stopped me, as well as not ending up in the deep of the Atlantic Ocean.

MIRACLES BEFORE TAKE OFF

I think there are two ways to fly first class: The first is being rich and wanting to spend that much money. The other is having the status of a high rank frequent flyer on some airline. In my case, I am at the maximum on both sides, I am a Platinum Executive traveler each year, and if I don't plan on travelling often, I am a Platinum AA Advantage traveler for life. That is to say, I have travelled more than two million miles just with American Airlines, so I don't need to travel much to qualify again. As a matter of fact, I don't have to fly at all and I am a member with Platinum Privileges for the rest of my life at American Airlines.

Now, that is the way to travel first class in the normal way, but there is another way which I personally discovered and have enjoyed on many occasions. That is the "supernatural" way. If someone opts not to believe in this option, don't worry, I won't be offended. Jesus clearly said, *"If thou can believe, all things are possible to him that believeth"* (Mark 9:23). Spoken another way, "If thou cannot believe, all things are impossible to him that believeth not." It has been possible for me to fly First Class and achieve many objectives in life, because I believe in the power of God.

The reason why I tell you all of these things (I will explain again), is not for vain glory. It is simply because I know who I am and where I come from. I am the son of country folk who was born on a remote mountain in Central America, without any inheritance or any apparent future of promise. However, in Christ I have had everything that was lacking, including achieving a life of splendor and gala.

MY FIRST FLIGHT
IN FIRST CLASS

I flew first class before I could depend on being a frequent flyer. Simply put, I desired it. I believed, and this one of a kind miracle presented itself to me. So that you will understand where I am coming from, I am going to share a few short episodes. I was coming from the Dominican Republic, after having seen the hand of God working powerfully and later daring to "ordain more than 2,000 youth as Ministers of Personal Evangelism." I performed the ceremony of ordination for all of them in a single day. The national Bishop of that Council of Churches authorized me to carry out the ceremony. That was under the condition that I tell people he did not officially authorize me, to avoid problems with his syndicates (although between us, he did permit me unofficially)... The whole event was a blessing. They had given me four, of the now extinct, "one cabin upgrade stickers" that are now electronic, which I wanted with all my heart, to fly home in First Class. I gave the upgrade stickers to the desk agent of American Airlines. He told me to present it at another counter. The person who attended me at the next place observed that I was wearing a very elegant suit. He looked at me from head to toe and for some reason, didn't like me, and he told me that there wasn't room and First class was completely full. I asked him to confirm that, as he hadn't even checked on the computer. I realized that this Hispanic receptionist was totally envious, but he confirmed, "Yes, there is room, but your ticket is one of the cheapest that exists and you don't qualify."

"Are you sure I don't qualify?" I asked. "You haven't even seen my ticket," I added.

"I know perfectly well what kind of ticket you have," he ended and turned to look another way.

NOBODY TAKES MY BLESSING AWAY!

Without a doubt, flying in First Class is not a primary need. In the end all the passengers arrive on the same flight and in the same place. However, I also believe that just like any good father, our God on many occasions is conscious of the whims of those children who can believe. I have found and emphasized that those miracles can only be received by those who believe and seek them. I remember how Jesus motivated us in the following way: *"Ask, and it shall be given you; seek, and ye shall find; knock, and it shall be opened unto you: For every one that asketh receiveth; and he that seeketh findeth; and to him that knocketh it shall be opened. Or what man is there of you, whom if his son ask bread, will he give him a stone? Or if he ask a fish, will he give him a serpent? If ye then, being evil, know how to give good gifts unto your children, how much more shall your Father which is in heaven give good things to them that ask him?"* (Matthew 7:7-11). If you don't ask, don't even seek the blessings of God, don't even knock on heaven's door, you will never see God working in that way. That's how it is, there is no discussion.

As a personal delight and something I inherited genetically from my dear father "Papa Cundo," I confess that I am very given to the fine or top quality life. Even though it doesn't matter to me if I sleep in the mountains on mission trips, it also doesn't make me uncomfortable when I can stay in the best hotels in the big cities. I confess that I don't live with great luxuries or commodities in my house, because I don't have money, I never have. Of course, when the opportunity comes, I live a life of gala with royalty, protocol and everything required for living the good life with little money…

Now then, dear readers of my blessed autobiography, rightly called "A Life of Miracles", what do you think happened? As much as that receptionist at the airport fought to keep me from flying first class, he couldn't. In the end, he had managed to get me a seat in the economic class in the tail of the plane. This was a well-chosen seat that I picked, in the aisle. For some reason closed in spaces affect me, it is some kind of claustrophobia and I can't stand them. For that reason, I almost never fly in a window seat, or in the middle. At first it didn't bother me, but now it does. What happened was, when I arrived at my seat, the flight attendant asked me, "Are you Mr. Vargas?" I replied affirmatively.

I'M SORRY SIR, BUT WE HAVE CHANGED YOUR SEAT

After identifying myself to the flight attendant as Mynor Vargas, she explained to me, "Forgive us, Mr. Vargas, we need to move you. This child is seated very far from his father. Originally the child was going to travel alone, but now his father is going with him, we need to seat them together."

I felt like the sky crashed down on earth. Not only had the envious man at the counter kept me from flying first class, but now they were moving me from the seat which I had carefully chosen. I was at the point of making some strong complaints to the stewardess, but I decided to keep silent and understand that the child needed to travel alongside his father. So I responded, "That seems fine, young lady. If it will help, I will happily move."

When she observed my friendliness and understanding, she smiled at me with a sweetness that I did not understand at first. I simply couldn't figure out why she kept looking at me and smiling over and over again. It was then that she asked, "Do you know where the child was sitting?"

I told her no, but it didn't matter, I would sit there. She continued:

"It is seat A1," she clarified. "You are going to first class," she ended.

I acted as if I was used to that kind of treatment. I, with all my style, took my new boarding pass and reciprocated the smile, and I said to her, "It is a great pleasure for me to help under these circumstances."

That final expression made the passengers in the neighboring seats laugh, and they made other funny comments and even applauded me.

I immediately began walking toward the front of the plane, where, as a Servant of God, I should be seated. At that time I did not drink any kind of wine as an appetizer or even for indigestion, what I did fill myself with was all the Coca Cola I could, and I ate everything they would give me. I also devoured the exquisite desert and traveled as if I was used to such sumptuousness. However, that was my first "first class trip" on a plane.

MY BROTHER SALVADOR, IS AN ANGEL

My brothers Salvador and Carlos are totally different than me. Their personal tastes, their conversations, their characters, ideas, and customs, are polar opposites from my own. However, we are identical in generosity and sense of humor and we get along very well. Salvador took me in his vehicle to the Boston airport. As much as I insisted on going from Providence, Rhode Island to Boston, Massachusetts on a bus line called Bonanza, that day that I was to travel to Lima, Peru, my brother Salvador insisted on taking me personally in his car. He understood perfectly the life of faith and my financial limitations. Just as we entered the famous Boston Callahan Tunnel, he asked me, "How are you? Are you happy? The long trip doesn't bother you?

I answered him, "No, to be honest, it doesn't bother me that the flight is long. I'm happy because I have upgrades so I can fly First Class on my first flight from Boston to Dallas."

"I'm glad," my brother said, but he emphasized how on the second flight, or the longer flight, I would be where all the poor are confined for the flight.

"Yes, but don't worry about that, I'll just sleep," I replied. What happened was that I flew the first flight in first class and I was just about to sit in the waiting room in the Dallas Airport, when I heard someone say in the loudspeakers. "Reverend Mynor Vargas, please come to the American Airlines desk."

The light bulb instantly went off and I thought, "That is my first class ticket." I got up and walked at a normal speed toward the counter. When I arrived, the young woman who attended me said,

"Please give me your boarding pass."

When I gave it to her, she took it and tore it into three pieces right under my nose, as I watched her attentively. After destroying my ticket, she gave me a totally new first class ticket. She did that without saying a single word to me. On my part, I just expressed,

"Thank you; this is just what I needed."

That day I was able to fly the way I desired. I think that it is important to know that in order to fly in first class from the United States to South America, one needs a lot of dollars ($$$) or an E-V.I.P. certificate which is only given to Platinum Executive travelers. I never asked on whose behalf or why the upgrade took place. But to be honest, I had been expecting that for a while. What I wanted was to travel comfortably so I could invest my strength in the great crusade that was to take place in Plaza de Toros in Trujillo, Peru.

MY NEPHEWS MOCKING ME

Today almost all the Vargas' travel in first class, but back then nobody did, absolutely nobody but me. Not even my brother the millionaire. Flying first class had nothing to do with money, but with taste and class.

One particular time we were flying from Guatemala City to Miami. I had commented several times before about the repeated occasions when I received courtesy upgrades to first class, and without realizing it I became an object of mockery in my family. My brothers did not like that I talked about it. One time when I was organizing a huge crusade my older brother came and rebuked me strongly for talking so much about my first class miracles. He said how without realizing it, I had become the object of mockery and discontent.

I found this out personally on this flight. When we arrived at the American Airlines desk, my nephews were making jokes about me, saying, "I can't wait to see uncle Mynor's first class seat." Some of them, when they arrived at the waiting room, put their fists to their mouths simulating a microphone and said, "Attention, your attention please, Dr. Vargas, Dr. Vargas, please come pick up your first class ticket at the American Airlines desk." They made one joke after another of this kind and everyone laughed hysterically. I could not help but to laugh with them, although inside I would have wanted to give a good slap on the head to those daring, mischievous boys.

I WAS RECOGNIZED AT THE GATE

The amount of flights I had taken to Guatemala was so many, that the flight attendants knew me. The trust was so high, that when a brand new plane arrived, they took me inside to see it before anyone else boarded. On this occasion, as all of the passengers were walking toward the inside of the plane, the stewardess recognized me and greeted me personally when I arrived at the first coach seat .

"Hello Mr. Vargas, it's good to see you. Where are you going today?"

I told her, "To Miami, and then Boston."

Right away, without looking at my seat number, she took my boarding pass and told me, "You are going to sit here." Once again it was seat "A1", my favorite seat on any flight. Another time, the famous and respected Global Evangelist Alberto Mottesi asked me if I was going to pilot the flight, because every time we see each other on flights, I am seated in chair "A1."

That day my nephews had to swallow their own jokes. They couldn't believe it, and I, with a slightly cruel attitude, remember what I said to them,

"Hey boys, please take good care of my bags. Ha, ha, ha, ha…"

It was payback time after they had made fun of me that morning; at least they got a taste of their own medicine. They didn't make fun of me about that again. Since then, they have been dedicated to tell everyone about how I, no matter where I go, always have the best seat. My little nephews are my life, I love them all the same and I feel like a father to them. The feeling and affection is returned by them. Let me clarify that, so that nobody misinterprets and thinks the Vargas' don't get along in reference to the jokes. That is in no way the case. Thank God, we are all joyful in total unity. Of course, we don't tolerate arrogance or anyone who thinks they are better than another. Maybe that feeling is what caused my beautiful nephews to believe that I was exaggerating about my life, flying in first class at the cost of being bumped down to economy class.

ARNOLD ENNS: YOU CAN NEVER WIN AGAINST GOD

This was the last trip of the famed and renowned Latin American Evangelist, Brother Paul, who traveled together with his wife Linda Finkenbinder. These beautiful, internationally renowned, elders had confessed to me that this would be their last trip to the International COICOM Congress. I had had the privilege of taking them to what would be their last Evangelistic Crusade, which took place in my home country of Guatemala, specifically in the birth place of my parents. I also took them to their last Evangelistic Service which took place in Providence, Rhode Island, the city where I have been located for many years. Now, for the third time, I had the privilege of taking them to their last Summit of Pastors and Christian Mass Media Communicators, COICOM. Brother Paul Finkenbinder practically never traveled again after this event. I knew the ending would have to be powerful. As we visited a mansion in Newport, Rhode Island, Bro. Paul and Linda began to tell me how difficult it was for them to travel because of their age. As a result, they would not go to COICOM 2008 in Panama City, Panama. I made them an offer they could not refuse. "Brother Paul, allow me to take care of your tickets which will be first class the whole way," I said. That would cost me four "E-VIP" certificates. Each one of those is worth $1,000.00. I also offered for Blanqui and I to travel from Boston to Los Angeles to be able to board the plane with them and accompany them for the entire trip. That meant I would be the assistant and bag boy for Paul and Linda along with my beloved wife Blanuzkia.

The offer was very tempting, and as a result Paul almost immediately said yes, they accepted. Of course, in giving away my four "E-VIP" certificates that implied that Blanqui and I would have to dare to fly across the entire continent of the United States of North America, and then Central America in economy class seats. All of that, to be able to give our First Class certificates to the fiery Patriarchs. My wife was totally submissive in that instance because to tell you the truth I never even consulted her. I made the decision alone and I gave my upgrades to the Finkenbinders. Ladies and gentlemen: said and done. When Brother Paul and Linda had their tickets bought, I called American Airlines and made the seat change. It was very easy because there was enough space available on the inventory for first class seats. Now, Blanqui and I continued confined in those regular seats, which after flying a distance of 15,000 miles, felt like chairs of steel.

The miracle happened when my friend Ruth Santiago, called my old colleague and friend, Reverend Jaime Najera, telling him that the wife of the famous multimillionaire artist Daddy Yankee, was giving away exactly four "E-VIP" certificates. My friend told her: "But I don't have any travel plans, so I don't need them, but let me see if Dr. Mynor Vargas needs them." When my colleague called me, I couldn't believe it, just five days before, I had given my valuable "E-VIP" upgrades to the servants of God, Paul and Linda Finkenbinder. Now, I was at the point of someone giving them to me. My dear readers let me tell you that not only did they give them to me, but there was space available in the first class cabin. So there we went, Paul, Linda, my Blanuzkia, and I in first class by the virtue of God. Hallelujah! God always gives us what we desire, always when there is no sin, or hurt toward anyone. I arrived in COICOM 2008 and I still couldn't believe it. I told the miracle to Lic. Arnold Enns, Executive President of COICOM and he told me, "Mynor, you can never out give God." And added, "When you sow in good soil, the harvest will be growing blessings."

In the end, as the old hymn says, "That same story, repeats itself again"... I have enough to tell you innumerable amounts of stories about first class flights at the price of a discount ticket or totally free, I could write a book completely about those kinds of stories. So we will leave that for now with concern to my testimony, but not in regard to yours.

Friend, my God is your God and if he can give me everything I need as well as a few other enjoyments; I am sure he can do the same with you. This is the day to decide to believe in a God who does not get angry when his children want the best. A God who is not disgusted to know that one of his Servants stayed in a first class hotel. The problem lies in the religiosity. I don't know who came up with the idea that Christians have to sit in the worst seats and sleep in the most deplorable places. If we are children of a God who has everything, who can do all things, and knows how to give good gifts and perfect presents to those who ask him (James 1:17), why then do we not ask him for these good gifts? On the contrary, it seems like we continue to be satisfied with crumbs.

For a square evangelical, there is nothing more beautiful than to see a brother who stays in a house or unpopular motel, while he does his Christian activities. Enough with the ignorance and absurd ideas! We can and will stay wherever is necessary. If today I have to sleep on a remote mountain with its weather, I will. If tomorrow they offer me a five star hotel, with the same joy I will go. Paul said, *"I know both how to be abased, and I know how to abound: everywhere and in all things I am instructed both to be full and to be hungry, both to abound and to suffer need"* (Philippians 4:12).

YOU RECIEVE WHAT YOU EXPECT

God desires to give you all the petitions of your heart (Psalm 37:4). If you dream big, you will receive big things. Now, if you prefer to stay small and hearty, then God will give you the desires of your heart. He is not going to take you by force or against your will to what is excellent, that is something you have to believe and accept. That is to say that you must choose the blessings in your own life: You can represent the person at the door asking for "A little offering for the love of God", or you can be the one who is standing at the door giving offerings to those who ask. It is time to place ourselves in the life and culture of the King and not of misery. God has called us to be the head and not the tail (Deuteronomy 28:13). The part at the back of the plane is called the tail and I refuse to go there. Therefore, although I never demand that somebody pay my first class tickets I always end up sitting there.

It does not matter if you don't work in a big company, what is important is your own faith. For example, you could have your own taxi; you could be the owner of a small business. There is a saying, "It is better to be the head of a mouse, than the tail of a lion." This is to say, it is better to be the head, whether of something big or small, but be at the front. If we live in holiness, and in obedience to the Word of God and exercise our faith, we will enjoy the Christian life in abundance (John 10:10). I noticed that of the five senses we have, four are in the head: sight, taste, smell, and hearing. Only one is in our hands: touch. That means that the head is the most important part of our body. We could lose both arms and both legs and be successful like the famous Australian motivator Nick Vukicic (if you don't know about him, I invite you to research him on the internet), but if we lose our head, we lose our life.

Don't forget: You are the head, and not of a mouse, but of a CHAMPION!

GIVING AN OPPORTUNITY TO A POTENTIAL LEADER

It was my second trip to Chicago, Illinois, and I was still very young. I was only 22 years old. However, I was very sought after, so much so that professionally I brought an assistant with me. This time, my aid was a person who at the same time, would receive from me the opportunity to preach for the first time. It was the apostle Walter Morales, better known as "Dynamite." Back then, Walter was just a recently converted worldly person and had been rehabilitated from drugs. There, miracles were multiplied, in the air as well as on earth.

I felt the need to travel with someone else, and so I opted to find a travel companion on this precious occasion. Being very young still, I sought someone older than myself, so they wouldn't just see two young guys and lose respect. On the other hand, if I brought a person who was an expert he could act like my boss and I WOULD IN NO WAY ACCEPT THAT. So I decided to invite a person who was recently converted and showed potential as an international preacher. I hadn't even finished inviting him when he replied,

"Yes, I'll go. I'll carry your bags, take pictures and video of you and assist you in whatever you want."

"No, you don't understand," I explained. "You're not only going as my assistant. You are also going as my companion. You are going as even more than that, as my associate, you are even going to preach a night of the Evangelistic Campaign," I added.

Walter couldn't believe it. Nobody had ever trusted him with the pulpit before. Walter had been a terror and the dishonor of his family in the past, but now the blood of Jesus had transformed him totally and absolutely. Many of my advisors warned me of the risk of taking a novice with a past like his. They named off other reverends who they suggested I bring instead of a new convert. As always though, I ended up using my free will and I did as planned. I have always thought that a good leader is one who forms other good leaders.

That once secular man, who is now an apostle of many churches in North, Central, and South America, was very excited. He was preaching to everyone he found in his path in the airport. I, as always, was very serene, elegant and stylish. Meanwhile he was passing out tracts left and right.

PAN AM EXPRESS FLIGHT: MIGUEL YOUR FATHER WILL LIVE

We boarded our first plane to New York where we would take another to Chicago. We hadn't even sat down when my companion began to preach. It was an express flight on the now extinct Pan American Airlines; it was on a modern two turbine jet. Therefore, I considered it time to delight in the short flight. My plans were to enjoy the moment. However, Walter decided to make a big scene preaching and testifying. For a moment I thought I had made a mistake bringing him with me. That plane hadn't even taken off when he had already given an evangelistic tract to the passenger sitting in front of us. The man turned around and said to us,

"I don't want anything. My father is dying in the Dominican Republic."

I already had my eyes closed and was trying to enjoy the comfort of the modern plane, when I heard Walter tell him, "You know, my friend sitting beside me can pray so your father doesn't die."

When I heard that, I almost died from shock. IT SEEMED INCONCEIVABLE TO ME! To me it was the straw that broke the camel's back. Not only did I have to deal with this chatterbox preaching beside me, but now he was alluding me as a healer and raiser of the dead. In an instant I realized that I would have to intervene. I said, "Sir, you should pray and believe that God will heal your father."
The dialogue took further shape when the man responded, "My father was stabbed several times by thieves last night and is on the brink of death."

He said this as he cried inconsolably. His tears bathed his face and poured out from behind his sunglasses. I felt a great deal of compassion for him and especially for his father. I admit that I did not feel like ministering or to preaching to him, I just wanted to enjoy my flight. But the need presented itself and sometimes you have to be willing to change your plans. Right there I felt the presence of God in all my being and without waiting one second more, I expressed a prophetic word, assuring him, "MIGUEL, YOUR FATHER WILL LIVE!!!"

I prayed with him, for him and for his father and I instructed him to buy a pair of shorts for the beach when he got home. He was to call his friends to go out and relax, because his father would not die. I was very specific in my instructions, and my faith worked in me in that moment of glory.

I AM A PROFESSIONAL BOXER

Some ten minutes after praying, the man turned around and told us, "It's all over."

He took off his dark sunglasses and expressed faith that his father would live. Later he gave us his business card and said, "I am a professional boxer. I split the face of anyone who lies to me or bothers me, but I like you guys and I believe in the prophecy that my father will live."

When I heard he was a boxer, I wanted to disappear from the plane. At least I hadn't given him my name. All that was left was for Walter Dynamite to pull another one of his stunts… He opened the briefcase he had and pulled out one of my business cards, which had my phone number and my home address. Walter had pure faith. There was no malice in him and he said to the professional boxer, "Here is my friend's card. If you need anything you contact him."

In that same instant I would have liked to be alone with Walter to grab him by the neck, but there were a lot of people around. It's true that when I prophesied, "Miguel, your father will live," I felt that it was from God. The anointing was so strong that I couldn't keep silent. However, I hesitated because at some point everyone has doubts. The father of the demon possessed boy said it best when Jesus asked him if he believed: *"Lord, I believe; help thou mine unbelief"* (Mark 9:24).

I believed that the man in the Dominican Republic would not die and I was totally sure in the word of faith I had given. But to give my card with my home address to a violent boxer was another story.

What happened was, a few weeks later, Miguel appeared at Walter's house, because I took it upon myself to give him Walter's phone number, address, and all the information I could. If there were any complaints, Walter would get what he deserved (ha, ha, ha, ha). The good thing is that God backed up his word, which asserts, *"with his stripes we are healed"* (Isaiah 53:5). The boxer stood before Walter to thank him and testify that the same day, like a master plan, even the same hour we were talking and praying in the plane, his father came out of his coma and spoke. He asked for food and began his recuperation. Instead of going to a funeral, Miguel enjoyed a nice vacation in his country.

BIG FISH IN THE NET

The miracles kept thriving. Morales preached in Chicago one of the nights, as was scheduled. When he gave the evangelistic invitation, five people came to the altar. Three of those people were powerful drug traffickers. One had a necklace worth more than $5,000.00 (at that time, $5,000 was a fortune). That same man had two Mercedes Benz and three Corvettes.

He also made a call for divine healing. I remember that I, as always, was praying with a lot of ethical and appropriate conduct while Walter, however, screamed in their ears and shook people. One woman came up with jaw problems. I prayed for her, but it seems like she didn't feel any flavor in my soft and formal manner.

When I finished praying, she opened her eyes and exclaimed, "I want the other guy to pray for me..."

One of the ushers said to her, "But Brother Mynor already prayed for you."

"Yes, but he didn't do it with any power, the other guy shakes you," she responded.

It was really funny to hear that the woman wanted him to shake her jaw, so I called Walter who came to the sick woman. He grabbed her, shook her, and screamed in her ear to receive divine healing. It was an explosion of spiritual dynamite as the woman started to be healed. How entertaining are the things that sometimes occur on such crusades! The important thing is that God was glorified in every message and in each testimony.

The reason why I set out to write these chronicles, including some minuscule facts, is the thought that readers like you need a miracle whether big or small. Jesus Christ is the same yesterday, today, and forever (Hebrews 13:8). In the same way Jesus did miracles in Chicago and in the air while we traveled toward the city, he wants to do a miracle in your favor today. I invite you to believe, ask, and receive in the powerful name of Jesus, amen.

Dr. Vargas praying among the people,
with the laying of hands.

Massive crusade in Llano Verde, Rio Hondo, Zacapa,
Guatemala (birth place of the Vargas family).

Pastors Mynor and Blanca Vargas day of Ordination
and Bishopric Endowment.

Dr. Vargas preaching in the Miracle Cathedral
(Entre Rios, Argentina).

Dr. Vargas in the Television Studio
of Global Evangelist Alberto Mottesi.

Mynor Vargas in New Life Worship Center.

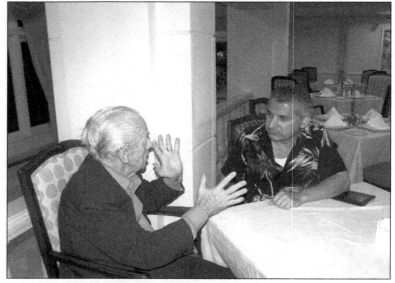

Mynor with his Mentor, the Apostle and Patriarch
Norman Parish in Guatemala.

Mynor with one of his Mentors,
Dr. Paul Finkenbinder, in California.

Father of Dr. Vargas, Mr. Jose Facundo Vargas Morales,
"Papa Cundo" (R.I.P.).

Dr. Moises Mercedes, Dr. Michael Pangio and Dr. Ernest
Gibson conferring a Doctor of Philosophy in Ministry,
Ph.D. to Dr. Vargas.

Dr. Vargas in his first ministerial steps,
using the clerical collar for a wedding ceremony.

Mother of Dr. Vargas, Mrs. Virgilia Berlamina
Oliva Roldan Vargas "Mama Mina" (R.I.P.)
and Mynor Vargas at age 5.

Mynor Vargas, evangelizing on a donkey on a remote
mountain in Zacapa, Guatemala, in 1989.

Dr. Mynor Vargas, flying first class on a transatlantic
flight on an American Airlines Boeing 777-200
in February 2010.

Pastors Mynor and Blanca on Christmas 2003.

During his time as International Evangelist,
Mynor Vargas was accustomed to praying for people,
while going into the multitude.

Anointing hundreds of Leaders and Pastors
for the holy ministry.

Mynor Vargas making a mixed call of reconciliation
and to work in the ministry of God.

Dr. Mynor Vargas preaching in a Massive Crusade in the
Ministry Hope of Life, organized by Carlos and Salvador
Vargas. Approximately 25,000 assisted during the five
nights of the Campaign.

Mynor Vargas as a Conference Speaker in Trujillo, Peru.
Three level auditorium completely filled with Ministers
and Pastors.

Mynor in the first office of the Ministry
"A Fragment of Hope" in the year 1985.

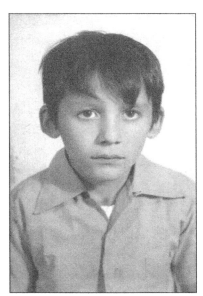

Mynor Vargas at age 7.
Photograph taken in April of 1973.

The family of Dr. Vargas: Sheyna, Gabriel, Blanca,
Mynor, Matthew, Jacob, Gabrielita and Mark.

The Vargas brothers in Guatemala with the ex-First Lady
of the nation, Mrs. Patricia de Arzu.

The Vargas brothers with the ex-Vice President of
Guatemala Dr. Luis Flores.

Mynor Vargas as an Evangelist praying for indigenous
people who accepted Jesus as savior.

Mynor y Blanca Vargas on the day of their wedding
(September 13, 1981).

Dr. Vargas, receiving the key to the city of Esperanza in
Trujillo, Peru, and being named Honorable Son by the
Municipal Mayor (Year 1995).

Mynor Vargas at the first COICOM (year 1992), which
took place in Santa Cruz de la Sierra, Bolivia.
Table of the founding members of COICOM presenting
ideas for ALAS (Latin America Via Satellite).

Dr. Vargas at the first FEXPOCOM
(Communicators Fair which takes place each COICOM)
with his exhibition table (year 1992).

Mynor at the first COICOM
in Santa Cruz of the Sierra, Bolivia (year 1992).

Lic. Victor Suchite, International Consultant
for Dr. Mynor Vargas and Norman Parish, Mentor.

Dr. Mynor Vargas, Bishop of the Shalom Consortium and Apostle to the Nations, preaching in his home town.

5

FINANCIAL MARACLES

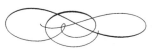

"It was time to pay the taxes in Capernaum, specifically the temple tax. The tax collectors came to Simon Peter, the most outstanding of the 12 disciples of Jesus and they asked him, "Does your Teacher pay the two drachmas?"
"Of course he does," was the response of the brave disciple. He had been a witness over and over again of how his Master complied in giving to Caesar what belonged to Caesar, and to God what belonged to God. With words and acts his Master had taught them to fulfill all financial commitments. This time was no exception. Peter went to find Jesus to inform him that they were waiting to receive the tax. However, when he entered the house, it was the Lord, who had the first word and asked his opinion,

"What do you think Peter? The kings of the earth, who do they collect taxes from, their own children or from strangers?"

"The strangers," Simon Peter responded immediately.

"Of course!" said Jesus, "The children of the kings are exempt from paying taxes." The message was clear. Jesus as the Son of God should not pay taxes, being the King of kings and Lord of lords. That day Jesus did not have a single cent in his pockets. So he sent Peter to do the following: "Even though I shouldn't pay taxes, since they don't know me, go to the sea. Take with your fishing hook with you and throw it in, the first fish you catch will have a coin in its mouth. Take the coin out of the fish's mouth and pay the taxes for you and I. That disciple followed faithfully the instructions of his Master. He went to the sea with a fishing pole on his shoulder. Trembling, he cast out the line. Some fisherman had lost a coin and it tended up at the bottom of the sea. A fish went and ate the coin, thinking it was food. The coin got stuck in its mouth. It went up and up, and soon it bit Peter's hook and was caught. He opened the fish's mouth and took out the coin right away. Peter knew the chances of finding a coin in the mouth of the first fish he caught were one in a hundred million. Therefore, it was a real miracle. He took the money to the tax collector and paid for them both."

The story I just shared with my strokes of imagination, comes from the Bible, specifically Matthew 17:24-27. Let us look at the sacred text, *"And when they were come to Capernaum, they that received tribute money came to Peter, and said, Doth not your master pay tribute? He saith, Yes. And when he was come into the house, Jesus prevented him, saying, What thinkest thou, Simon? of whom do the kings of the earth take custom or tribute? Of their own children, or of strangers? Peter saith unto him, Of strangers. Jesus saith unto him, Then are the children free. Notwithstanding, lest we should offend them, go thou to the sea, and cast an hook, and take up the fish that first cometh up; and when thou hast opened his mouth, thou shalt find a piece of money: that take, and give unto them for me and thee."* Personally I think that it is unlikely today that God would provide money miraculously through the mouth of a fish, but in my life he has done it in many equally miraculous or extraordinary ways. I will share some of them with you in this chapter:

LORD! GIVE ME A FIXED INCOME WITHOUT HAVING TO WORK

That was the prayer I lifted up to my God over and over again when I was approximately 22 years old. I asked this of God first of all because I found myself in a tremendous financial decline. Secondly, I had multiple occupations that didn't allow me to seek a job in a company. Humanly speaking, there was no solution to that difficult situation. I needed a fixed income, an extra salary, but I could not commit myself to another job for lack of time
.

During that time I was already serving the Lord. I was taking my first steps as an International Evangelist, but I didn't do it full time. One day I exercised my faith and I spoke honestly with God, "Lord, I need a job but it can't be during the first shift, or the second shift, or the third shift. You know that it can't be the first shift (from 7:00 a.m. to 4:00 p.m.) because I have to attend to my gardening business. It can't be the second shift (4:00 to 12:00 pm) because I have to attend to the things of the Ministry. It can't be the third shift (12:00 p.m. to 6:00 a.m.) because I have to sleep. Do a miracle Lord! Give me a job, another fixed income, without having to work! My God, I am busy 24 hours a day, but I also have a need for money. Provide a job for me that will not interfere with my activities in those hours. I don't know how you will do it, but I am sure that nothing is impossible for you. In Jesus name Amen."

That prayer did not seem to make sense, but it was full of faith. The next day I got my hands on the newspaper called the "The Providence Journal Bulletin" and I went directly to the want ads. I continued exercising my faith, believing that something would appear. I found that the Ocean State Janitorial Company, Inc. was looking for employees. I went to the office and spoke with the owner, Mr. David Agostini, and I told him,

"I need a job urgently."

That man looked me head to toe and responded, "There are no more positions they've all been taken."

I asked him to please make sure that was the case. He responded one more time,

"There is nothing available."

When I was about to leave after saying thanks, he called me and asked me if I would be willing to take a third shift working as a security guard in a luxurious mall. I immediately thought that meant working every night without sleep. I was at the point of turning it down, but later I gathered my confidence in God and accepted.

I took the job and presented myself at the mall that same night. It was a luxurious mini mall, called Cohoes Commons in Garden City, where a lamp with more than 5,000 lights adorned each hallway. It was terrible, I struggled with sleep but I managed to finish that first night. When I left there, my gardening job was waiting for me, afterward ministry, spending time with family, and back to security guard. Throughout the week I only slept two or three hours during the afternoons. I was at the point of quitting the security job when something interesting happened. One night I fell into a deep sleep and I didn't wake up for the entire shift. Obviously I had several hours of lost sleep built up in my body and sooner or later it had to be regained. That night, David, my immediate boss (not the owner, but a guy with the same name), arrived to supervise, but he found me in such a deep sleep that he didn't wake me and I didn't even realize he had visited. Naturally my boss passed the report onto the owner, and even though he was just fulfilling his responsibility, he did it in a wrong way. He should have warned me before reporting me. The owner asked me to come to his office. It took me two days to answer his calls and present myself in his office because I thought he was going to fire me. Finally I arrived before him. To my surprise he said,

"Do you have any idea how special the job I gave you is? Do you know what this is about?"

When I heard those questions, I thought those would be his last words. To my bewilderment, he continued,

"This job is not for you to go to work, or pass sleepless nights. The job you have is simply to come and sleep every night in this building." Later he added, "Go into the pantry in the back room and you can sleep comfortably and safely. In the case that a thief does come in, just pick up the phone and call the police."

In reality, that entire building was protected with modern alarms and police that constantly circled the place, so there was no reason to stay awake. I earned $335.26 a week, just to go sleep for seven hours a night in that place. I did that for a year and a half. I should clarify that this was 24 years ago, and back then that amount of money is now equal a lot of dollars today. All of that money was just to sleep comfortably and safely in a secret room. You tell me, my dear reader, is that not a miracle? Wasn't it a precise answer from God? I was able to easily get out of my financial problems and continue serving my God faithfully, thanks to that wonderful miracle. Remember that "a miracle is an event caused by God, outside the limits of natural law, with the purpose of reinforcing His Word or benefiting one, or several persons." God worked that miracle with the purpose of benefiting me and to honor my faith. Hebrews 11:1 says, *"Now faith is the substance of things hoped for, the evidence of things not seen."* I had the certainty that God could give me a fixed salary without the need to work, and God did it.

THE FIRST COICOM

God has allowed me to be present in historic events, which have been written in the history books of Christianity, such as the foundation of COICOM. After having been faithful and obedient to invest all the money I had, even though I didn't have enough to pay for my own events, "CERCC 89" (The Christian Communicators Summit) and "CERCC 91", God in his sovereign will, prepared and made everything possible for me to be present in the "Santa Cruz 92" Summit. It was there in Santa Cruz de la Sierra, Bolivia, where what is known as "The First COICOM" happened. Out of nowhere, the same jungle boy from the hovels, the son of a country man and boy who didn't go to school, ended up being one of the 78 founders of the Latin American Confederation of Christian Communicators and Mass Media. COICOM is the largest entity in the Latin American world in respect to mass communication of Christian media. COICOM is the equivalent of the NRB (National Religious Broadcasters); the only difference is that it has a much wider reach when it comes to the number of countries. My role in this recognized organization is that of "Founding Member." I did not give myself this title; it was given to me by the organizers. From the central offices, I received a letter where it said that had been decided. It is a letter that I still have today in my safe-box. The correspondence said that its recipient was a "Founding Member of COICOM." To me, that's a wonder, because I don't think I am worthy or competent of such a great privilege. Today I continue to be part of COICOM, in the little that I have been able to, I have served two terms as part of the Executive Board and in several years of this congress I have been an Official Gold Sponsor. I assist every year and I see COICOM as something sacred and worthy of much respect.

FINANCES TO TRAVEL TO SANTA CRUZ

The miracle was not just that I was there at the first COICOM, and that I am a founding member, the best is still to be described. A month before, I did not have a single penny to go to the event. However, my trip had been confirmed a long time before and I had no intention of cancelling it. Two weeks before the date of the event, my economic situation had not changed. I simply had no money, but my plans to go and participate, were still intact. There was one week left, then five days, three days and nothing happened. NOTHING! I should say that my plane ticket was paid for either by exchanging frequent flyer miles, or maybe I bought it with a credit card, honestly I don't remember how I paid. What is for sure is that of the money to pay for the hotel, food, event registration and other costs, I HAD NOTHING!!

A day before the trip there wasn't so much as a smoke signal. Maybe 18 hours before, I still had nothing, and I thought for sure I was going to travel with empty pockets as I had on other occasions. I thought I would see the miracle at the place in question. Thank God, at 3 in the afternoon (12 hours before leaving) someone came to my house, knocked on the door and told my wife that he was in a hurry but he needed to leave an envelope for Brother Mynor because he was going to Bolivia. To this day I don't know who told that person my plans, because I hadn't said anything to anyone; but that was the first miracle which was a divine sign. The envelope had $60.00 which represented 1% of what I would receive over the next 12 miraculous hours. It seems completely incredible, but after that person, another arrived, and later another, after that another and another, etc., etc., etc. Each one came with an offering in their hand or in an envelope for my trip. I have to add that in that time there wasn't email, and I didn't do any kind of publicity campaign. If I had made big announcements and publicized my trip, it wouldn't be a miracle; it would be a marketing success. Imagine that there were times when I just heard someone talking outside of my house depositing something in my mailbox. When I went to look, there was an offering in it. One after another came with money and I put it in my thin, plastic, obscurely beige colored briefcase. I was very happy, and I don't know why but I did not open a single one of those envelopes as they arrived. All I did was put them in the briefcase. To top it all off, there was someone who came at 12 at night and gave me their offering. Who had made this announcement? NOBODY! Absolutely no one in the natural world. To this day I still don't know how it happened. There's more, it had never happened before and nothing like it has ever happened to me since.

DO I SLEEP OR COUNT THE MONEY?

I was doing the last check of my luggage when I realized that it was 2:00 a.m. and in an hour I had to leave for Logan Airport in Boston where I would take my first flight. What should I do? Should I sleep a mere hour or count the money? To tell you the truth, there is something that fascinates every evangelist living entirely by faith: counting the offering, and receiving the offering. So I started opening each envelope and counted all the money. You might not believe it, my beloved reader, but the sum exceeded more than $6,000.00. That money made me rich for a week. However, all was used for my costs and to bless others who arrived without any money, including six young Chileans who came by bus to Santa Cruz. I remember my joy in sharing was so great, that on the last day of the Congress, when we had free time to go buy gifts and souvenirs, I called the Chilean youth and gave them $60.00 each so they could buy as well. At that moment the person who was the elected secretary of COICOM was there, and he watched me when I gave out the money. I just noticed that he made a gesture with his head and then smiled. I don't know if he did it approving or disapproving of my action. What was certain is that I was more interested in exercising my gift of giving than anything else.

15 YEARS AFTER COICOM

As we celebrated the 15th anniversary of COICOM, Lic. Raul Justiniano, founder and president of the organization, was asked about the memories he had of things that most stood out in regard to the foundation. He said the following: "I remember when Mynor Vargas arrived, he was just a kid. His hair was still black without a single grey one. He had a big roll of money and he went around giving it away to everyone." Justiniano added more details, "When somebody opened the door for him, he gave them a Washington (that's what he calls dollars), the same when someone carried his bag; another Washington when they brought him food, and even when they greeted him. He was giving Washington's to everyone who stepped in front of him… " He expressed that at the gala dinner in front of hundreds of Presidents of Ministries and Mass Media from about 30 countries. To this day I realize that my deeds of generosity have become notorious, and I thought that only a few people had observed them. I arrived at the first COICOM acting like a "millionaire" without anyone knowing that the day before I didn't even have enough for a hot dog. God is always faithful with me. Hallelujah, amen.

I WAS LEFT WITH NOTHING BUT FAITH

The last of the miracles in that first COICOM that I register and confess, occurred on the flight back. Being there I gave away everything I had, so much so, that the young "Alejandro," who helped me so well and assisted me professionally during the whole Congress, did not receive everything I wanted to give him (how embarrassing… I should have never left him to be the last person I gave an offering to).

I was on my way on the plane, literally with no money. My gift of giving was so big, and the impulse to do so, that on that occasion I forgot to buy souvenirs for my wife, children, and parents who were still alive. "Now what do I do?" I asked myself as I flew from Santa Cruz de la Sierra, Bolivia, to Miami, Florida, which was my port of entry. "I have no money, and debts are waiting for me." During the Congress I had forgotten that the day after my arrival I had to pay $700.00 for a previously acquired commitment. How could I be so barbaric and spend and give away everything? There on the plane, I felt like crying, but instead of that I started to pray. I experienced so much faith while I prayed, that I declared a miracle in my bank account. I had seen God work before and I could not doubt on this occasion. I took my blue colored debit card from the now disappeared "Fleet National Bank" in my hand, and I pronounced audibly the following declaration: "When I arrive in Miami I will go to the ATM and there will be $60.00 to by souvenirs for my family." That would have been possible only by a miracle, because the night before my trip I had taken out everything the ATM allowed me and almost everything that I had in the account, and later, on the morning of my trip I withdrew money again, I took out the rest. The account was left completely empty.

MONEY WITHOUT EXPLANATION

We all know that faith without works is dead (James 2:20). The prayer had been made in the plane and received at the throne of grace. Now comes the most interesting part, as I walked toward the ATM to take out money. We all know that an ATM will not give out a single cent if there is no cash available in the account. I hoped there would not be anyone around the machine. I got my card ready to insert when other people arrived to do the same thing. I politely let them go ahead of me (in reality I didn't want them to see me nervous). After everyone had taken money out, I came close to the ATM again. I prayed a brief prayer in my mind while I put in the PIN and asked for a bank statement. You won't believe it but I had a cold sweat

on that occasion. It couldn't fail; I was standing with
a declaration of faith and the debit card had to give me
everything I needed or I was going to need an explanation.
For some reason it didn't give me the receipt that tells
the balance of the account. I got even more nervous. I
thought that it had swallowed my card and I would never
get it back... However it immediately expelled it. I felt
like it had spit in my face. After taking it I thought about
just going to my gate to board my last plane and forget the
whole thing. At that point I had a line of people behind
me, so I got out of the way. All I could do was watch as
one by one they took out 20, 40 and even $100.00. I felt
like I was drooling when I saw those bills. It was then that
I armed myself with faith again and when the people left, I
went back to that blessed ATM. This time I didn't ask for
the bank statement, I just asked for the $60.00 which I had
prayed for on the plane. Glory to God for what happened!
To my surprise, not only did it give me the $60.00 that
I needed for my families' souvenirs, but the screen also
showed me a balance of $704.00. "That is impossible!" I
thought. I had left with everything that was in my account
a week before. I had not made a single deposit, it was
totally impossible. But fine, the issue is that there was
money in the account for that amount and I remembered
that the next day I had to pay exactly $700.00. I remember
that I stood with a millionaire style and I showed off a little
so the people behind me would observe how the machine
gave me bill after bill of this great sum of money. Now
things had changed. It was the other people who watched,
who had drool running down their mouths at the sound of
the machine counting off the bills (ha, ha, ha, ha). I can't
stop laughing because life is beautiful and even though we
pass through storms, God is always there to help us, and
he doesn't let us perish. The story ends with me having
enough money to bring back gifts to my wife, my children
and my parents. That same week I went to the bank to

see what had happened after I left for Bolivia. I asked for a bank statement and found that it showed that one day after I had traveled to Bolivia there was a deposit to my account. I don't know who did it, nobody, nobody, NOBODY knew my bank account number and as much as I tried, the bank did not give me an explanation, so I didn't pursue it. The truth is, it really didn't interest me anymore. The important thing is that I continue believing that it was God who performed one more miracle for the glory of his name.

I DON'T KNOW IF IT WAS A MAN OR AN ANGEL

I do not exaggerate in saying that to this day, I have my doubts. I give a 50/50 chance and I continue trying to analyze if it was an angel or a country man. What am I talking about? Let me explain: It happened about 18 years ago. I was coming from an event that was explosive and full of faith at Oral Roberts University. The event was ICBM (International Charismatic Biblical Ministries). I attended with much faith, investing what I had and even what I didn't have and using credit cards. My hunger for the supernatural carried me to continue learning from the great evangelists of our time. There I met and spoke in person with the famous prosperity preacher, Robert Tilton and with the honorable Nigerian preacher, Benson Idahosa. The first of them is not on the same ministerial scale now. The second is resting in the presence of the Lord.

The issue is that during the whole week I heard big things spoken of, from people who had already achieved them. At that same event I was personally ministered to by Billy Joe Daugherty, Pastor of the "Victory Outreach" mega

church WITH 17,000 MEMBERS and founder of 535
biblical institutes around the world (Billy is also with the
Lord, which is much better for him). Nothing compares
to that Summit. Among other great Servants of God who
ministered there, was Oral Roberts, Richard Roberts,
Joyce Meyer, etc. In the end, the cast was unbeatable;
they all had true ministries of faith and moved millions
of dollars. I was just a dreamer and a child of faith.
The significance for me was not what I had or what I
could obtain in amounts of money and crowds, but what
mattered to me was the Word of power that I would learn.
I end this paragraph by telling you about Peter J. Daniels,
one of the biggest millionaires in Australia and even still
in the world who appears in Wikipedia as a tycoon. There
were three long, but amazing seminars, each two hours
long. There I learned, among many other things, that
every vision or project should be written in a minimum
of 50 pages along with an achievement plan with desired
goals clearly mapped out. I bought three books by Peter
J. Daniel including the Best Seller *"How to Reach Your
Life Goals."* After that I bought all of his study programs,
some of them cost $1,200, $800.00 and $700.00 each
video packet and audio book.

Now, back to my enigma about the matter of "whether it
was a man or an angel"... Remember that's how this section
started? I had a wonderful experience after meeting all of
these great Generals of Christ of the modern age. The
following week I had to leave for the Dominican Republic
to fulfill a commitment I had made with a lot of anticipation.
At that time the Chancellor of the Evangelical University
of the Dominican Republic, the Reverend Danilo Grullon,
had asked me to participate in a tour of six cities, which
they called the "Theological Counsel of Church Growth." I
accepted their invitation without discussing the conditions
of things like payment of airfare, housing and much less

honorarium fees. The situation is that the date arrived for the trip and nobody informed me about the purchase of my tickets, hotel reservations, or anything. The only thing I knew was what was in my schedule; I had a commitment to fulfill. The ticket had been bought before, but once again I didn't have a cent on me. The insufficient $126.00 I managed to gather was used in the following way: I left $100.00 with my wife Blanqui and I brought $26.00 in my pocket. I didn't even know where I was going, or where I would sleep. When I left the airport, a couple of attentive youth picked me up and drove me to the home of the distinguished pastor Braulio Portes. They told me when we arrived that it would be my house, and I should feel in total confidence to use whatever I wanted. The only thing was that I would cook my own food, because they had a very busy schedule with the university, work, etc. It was a pleasure for me to cook my own food.

In that place I was only supposed to stay two days (the first and the last of the trip), the rest of the time I was to be traveling to different cities sharing in the conferences of the Theological Council. The other houses where I stayed, did not offer basic commodities.

As I remember, I traveled to this country in the Caribbean with only $26.00 in my pocket. Let me tell you how they started to disappear before I arrived at the house of Mr. Braulio Portes. First, I had to give a 5 dollar tip to the baggage handler of American Airlines in Providence, Rhode Island; and afterward, 5 dollars more to the first baggage handler in Santo Domingo. This man walked with me a few meters down the road until we arrived at a certain door; he told me that his jurisdiction only allowed him to carry the bags to that place. So a companion of his took my bags the rest of the way. After he did that I took $5.00 and gave the tip to the first of them. At that point, only $16.00 were left in my pocket. When we arrived at the car, the baggage handler said I had been served and he had to go, leaving the bags beside the car. Once again I did the obvious. I gave him $5.00, leaving me with $11.00 in my pocket. Before I could place a hand on one of my bags to put it in the trunk, without realizing it, another baggage handler appeared out of nowhere, took my bags and put them in the car. He told me that was his job, to put the bags in the car for me. There went another $5.00, leaving me with a scant $6.00 in my pocket. I got into the car quickly before another baggage handler could appear and take the last of what I had. Once I closed the car door I felt safe, but now all I had was $6.00 for food. However, the window was open and someone came up to it. It was a homeless man approximately 40 years old, who said to me, "You are coming from the United States and I have nothing to eat, please, give me some of your abundant money." I did not know what to do, whether to confess my misery or give him the money. Something happened inside me. I remembered how I had just been with those great champions of faith at Oral Roberts University and with a friendly smile I told him, "Of course my friend, giving to you is a blessing to me." Ladies and gentlemen, I took out the last $6.00 in my pocket, and gave them to that unfortunate homeless man, converting him instantly into a richer man than I. Of course, in giving him that money, I was accepting his words as a prophecy when he said, "Give me some of your abundant money"...

When the car started down the road, I couldn't believe it, I felt like a millionaire without a single dollar in my pocket. The young men, who arrived to pick me up, admired my generosity.

They imagined that the International Conference Speaker came loaded with money. They did not imagine that the reality was just the opposite; I had given everything and I didn't have enough for anything.

Okay, you have patiently followed me through the story up to now. It is time to tell you about the mysterious person who could have been an angel or a country man. I found myself in the second city doing conferences, I felt God present and backing me up with a very powerful Word and A LOT OF ANOINTING! Someone showed me in secret, the evaluation forms the assistants filled out and I came out as the favorite speaker by the audience. At the end of that second day of activities, a man came up to me. He was in a huge group of people that were greeting me and asking me questions. He asked me, "Brother Mynor, would you let me give you a hug?" I thought about it for a millisecond, the man was from the country, dressed in a short sleeve lime green shirt and moss green pants. He had tangled hair; he was sweaty with bits of moss or grass all over his clothes, arms and even his face. I was in a sky blue, three piece suit with a white shirt and tie which I had just gotten back from the dry cleaner. Now this sweaty, dirty man, with pieces of pasture and bark on his clothes, asks me for a hug... As I said earlier, I did not think about it for more than a millisecond and I said to him, "With pleasure my friend and brother, WITH PLEASURE!" There is more to it. I asked the people to make way, and I walked down the steps of the pulpit and went to give him a "bear hug." I felt so blessed by God and I had so much faith that not even a millionaire could feel as sure of himself as I did. After giving him a long, warm hug, the man said to me, "Your message was very good, thank you for coming to my people." Afterward he took some money out of his pocket and said to me, "This will help you." He immediately turned around and left.

COUNTRY MAN OR ANGEL?

When we were on our way back to the house where I would sleep that night, I told the young men who drove me in the oldest, run down car I have ever been in in my life, to take me to a place where I could buy a Coca Cola. They asked me to forgive them, but that they could only do it if I had money for it; otherwise no, because they didn't have any money themselves. I immediately replied, "Yes, I have some; a man from the country gave me an offering." They asked me, "How much could it be? Here the offerings aren't enough for even a single Coca Cola." I took the money out of my pocket and I stammered some jargon, what any good neo-Pentecostal and charismatic would understand to be angelic tongues (glosalia). The boys turned around to look at me in the back seat, as I informed them, "It's $400.00." Instantly the driver slammed on the brake, causing the tires to screech on the asphalt.

Once he had the car at a complete stop he said, "Make sure, because it would be impossible for any country man to have that amount of money, and even less likely that it be in American dollars."

There was a moment of silence and then laughter. We laughed so much that our eyes shined with the amount of joyful tears. We couldn't believe it. They asked for information about the donor but nobody knew him. The next day, the news had turned it into A WHOLE SCANDAL! They informed the authorities of the Evangelical University of the Dominican Republic and the host church so they would investigate who the generous country man was. The biggest surprise was that not only could they not figure out who the person was, but NOBODY REMEMBERED EVER SEEING HIM BEFORE OR AFTER! After asking me about the details of that person, nobody remembered seeing me talking to the sweaty country man in lime and moss green colored clothes. Even though the whole time I was cared for by attentive assistants, none of them had any memory of me talking with this person.

THE MIRACLE WAS MINE

Is it possible that I am the only person who saw it? It is possible, very possible. However, the miracle was mine! I was in urgent need of divine intervention, because I had felt bad for not having any money. I remember very well how that person said to me, "Thank you for coming to my people." I believe that it could have been the angel of the Lord himself, people are his creatures and not of anyone else. Money in dollars is not what is used in that place, much less the amount of $400.00. Each one is at freedom to believe what they consider best as I continue believing that the possibilities are 50/50, as to whether it was an angel or a country man. One day in that eternal dawn I will ask Jesus who that nice person was who gave me money to eat with. Jesus will confirm to me whether it was a country man or an angel.

The miracle did not end there. Because of all of this, the Reverend Danilo Grullon, Chancellor of the University learned that I had been traveling with empty pockets, and he sent me $60.00 so I would have something. When I arrived at the next city, everyone knew that the International Conference Speaker didn't have a cent before, and possibly an angel had given me money, so everyone gave me an offering (ha, ha, ha, ha). I couldn't believe it, but I went back home with a lot of financial fruit; all for being obedient to God in going to fulfill the commitment to preach that I had made. Understand as well that God blessed me for giving everything I had to the homeless man at the airport. I didn't give him my last drachma; I gave him my last six greens.

My dear reader, God does not leave us with nothing. He sends us down mysterious trails and has us pass through waters that seem like they will drown us, but even in those precarious situations, he does not sleep. He just gives us a few minutes of loneliness to see how much faith we have.

Hebrews 11:6 says the following, *"Without faith it is impossible to be well-pleasing unto him; for he that cometh to God must believe that he is, and that he is a rewarder of them that seek after him."* When you and I set out to fulfill our calling and divine purpose, he sets out to provide everything we lack. There's more, as I write this autobiography that describes a life of faith and miracles, I don't know where I will get the money to do the first printing of the book in English and Spanish which you have in your hands. I don't know how I will pay my team of writers, editors and translators. I am less sure how I will obtain the money to pay for the printing of what will be thousands of books, equaling thousands of dollars. I don't know where the money will come from, all I know is that I must write about the wonders of the Lord and testify that he is the same yesterday, today and forever (Hebrews 13:8). What I also know is that if you are reading this autobiography it is because God worked another financial miracle in my life.

AND HOW ARE YOU?

Dear reader, my book is written thinking of you. I have lived an innumerable number of miracles, and I will continue believing and living "A Life of Miracles" until

God calls me to that sweet and eternal home. Because of that, I am interested in knowing, how you are? Are you going through some particular need that requires the supernatural intervention of God in your favor? Is there some situation out of your reach that only a miraculous hand can save you from? This is the day for you to believe and receive a miracle. I want to encourage you and ask you to believe and receive your wonder. Do not leave it for tomorrow or for when the situation has gotten worse. Today is the day to receive the blessing. I believe and I ask for it in the name of Jesus, amen.

6

LITTLE BIG MIRACLES

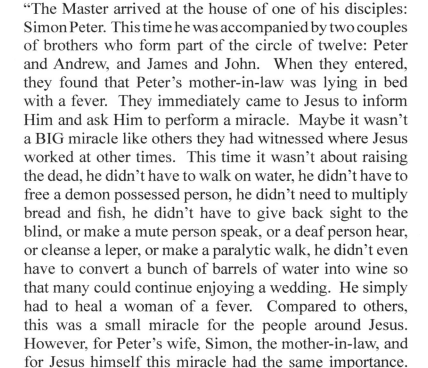

"The Master arrived at the house of one of his disciples: Simon Peter. This time he was accompanied by two couples of brothers who form part of the circle of twelve: Peter and Andrew, and James and John. When they entered, they found that Peter's mother-in-law was lying in bed with a fever. They immediately came to Jesus to inform Him and ask Him to perform a miracle. Maybe it wasn't a BIG miracle like others they had witnessed where Jesus worked at other times. This time it wasn't about raising the dead, he didn't have to walk on water, he didn't have to free a demon possessed person, he didn't need to multiply bread and fish, he didn't have to give back sight to the blind, or make a mute person speak, or a deaf person hear, or cleanse a leper, or make a paralytic walk, he didn't even have to convert a bunch of barrels of water into wine so that many could continue enjoying a wedding. He simply had to heal a woman of a fever. Compared to others, this was a small miracle for the people around Jesus. However, for Peter's wife, Simon, the mother-in-law, and for Jesus himself this miracle had the same importance. Jesus knew that he did not classify sins as big or small. He also didn't categorize miracles that way. Therefore, he came near to the bed where the woman laid, as the doctor, Luke indicated she had *"an immense fever"* (Luke 4:38)

and he took her hand. Without a doubt, Jesus felt that she had a fever of at least 103 degrees Fahrenheit, possibly provoked by a bacterial infection, or a virus. The Lord *"rebuked the fever"* (Luke 4:39), he lifted that woman and in an instant the infection, the bacteria or the virus, and the fever left. Peter's mother-in-law thanked Jesus, not just with words, but with acts. She went to the kitchen, put on her apron, prepared a delicious soup, and served them."

The story that you just read is a biblical and true story which is told in three of the four gospels: Matthew 8:14-17, Mark 1:29-31 and Luke 4:38-40. We see how the evangelist Mark tells it, but we will extend the text to verse 34: *"And straightway, when they were come out of the synagogue, they came into the house of Simon and Andrew, with James and John. Now Simon's wife's mother lay sick of a fever; and straightway they tell him of her: and he came and took her by the hand, and raised her up; and the fever left her, and she ministered unto them. And at even, when the sun did set, they brought unto him all that were sick, and them that were possessed with demons. And all the city was gathered together at the door. And he healed many that were sick with divers diseases, and cast out many demons; and he suffered not the demons to speak, because they knew him."*

Note that at the end of this long day, when night arrived, many people from that region crowded the doorway of Peter's house. People who had sick and demon possessed family members brought them so Jesus would heal them. The Lord healed many of them with diverse illnesses and cast out many demons. Once again: Surely the healing of Peter's mother-in-law's fever seemed like a small miracle compared to the others Jesus did at the end of that day.

SMALL BUT SIGNIFICANT

In the current chapter I will share what some may call "small miracles in the life of Mynor Vargas." To me, all miracles are big. A miracle is a miracle! For that, although it sounds paradoxical I have titled this section: "Little BIG miracles."

A miracle is a miracle and it doesn't matter how small it has been. It could have occurred in a moment so important, that the recipient may consider it to be the biggest of them all. In this chapter I will tell you some of the most chilling and phenomenal wonders that have happened in my life and have left me perplexed. I warn you that as small as they may seem, they will seem difficult to believe. However, as difficult as it is to believe them, they are as true as the sunlight that shines every day. Hallelujah, glory be to the name of Godd

FIVE CENTS FOR THE BUS

There are episodes in my present life, where I have had the need to gather many thousands of dollars to get out of a tight spot because of challenges and projects I have acquired. When my brothers and sisters ask me, "How much do you need?" I usually tell them, "I need five cents for the bus." I should clarify that in Guatemala we call the urban transportation "Buses." They know what I mean by my response, but I am sure that you still don't know my dear reader. For that reason, let me tell you about what I call the biggest miracle that has occurred to me, after my salvation. At many conferences I have proclaimed that this is the most significant and largest financial miracle that I have seen. Even though economically speaking it wasn't much, it had huge value in that it was the first time God provided finances for me just in time.

It was a beautiful day, approximately 32 years ago. I was 13 years old and I was already working for a mega-hardware-store selling construction materials, called 'Aldana Hermanos y Cia. Ltda.' That is the business where my father was the General Manager, the highest position the business had and the place where almost all of my father's children worked, with the exception of Lety, my youngest sister.

Mr. Augusto, owner of the central branch located in the Terminal of Zone 4, said to my father, "Cundo, your son should go to school." I refused to go to school because I wanted to have money to buy my clothes and the other needs of a young man of that age. So it was decided that they would send me to study part time. I enrolled into the IGA (Guatemalan American Institute). The money I earned would be adjusted so that I would not lose a single cent or waste anything; because that could only be the beginning of a catastrophe… I don't know exactly how it occurred, I don't remember very well, but from one moment to another, because of a stupid thing that has nothing to do with this particular story, I did not have the "five cents for the bus." In those days the urban transportation in Guatemala was the most economical in all of Latin America; it only cost 5 cents of a quetzal (the national currency).

I found myself very far from where I lived (14 Kilometers), and all I needed was 5 cents to get on the bus that would take me home. The ironic part of the situation is that even though what I needed was so little, without that fee I couldn't get on the bus. Being that as it was, I decided that I had better start walking. Even though it would take many hours walking, I would eventually get home. After a long time, I felt like my feet could give no more. I was just a boy; I didn't know what to do. All of a sudden, I remembered that when my mother took me to church, they talked about miracles. I immediately looked up at heaven, physically lifting my eyes upward, and I prayed to God asking him for what would come to be the biggest financial miracle recorded in my life.

In my prayer I asked God for a miracle, which later made me ask for a bigger one, and then later a much bigger one. I will explain: I prayed to God saying something like this, *"Lord, you are all powerful and I need a miracle. I need five cents so I can take the bus to get home. I can't walk anymore, I'm tired. Please do a miracle for me and give me five cents."* That time of prayer was so powerful for me, that in that moment I could almost touch the faith and the miracle it was set on. It was so much so that when I finished my prayer, I said within myself, "If God can give me five cents, he can also give me ten cents, that way I won't go in a regular bus, but the special one." As soon as that idea jumped in my mind, I corrected my prayer and said to God, *"Lord, if you can give me five cents, you can give me ten; so I would rather ask for ten so I don't have to go on the common bus, but on the special bus."* The prayer was completed, when right away I had an impulse of faith and expectation and just before finishing I thought within myself again, "If God can give me ten cents, it would be better to have fifteen, that way not only will I get to go on the special bus, but when I get off at the bus stop, I can buy two crunchy tortillas (tostadas), one with guacamole and the other with tomato salsa" (that is very typical in Guatemala). Dear reader, I do not lie or exaggerate when I tell you that the prayer was once again corrected and I said, *"GREAT AND ALL POWERFUL God, I know that you can give me five cents, just like you can give me ten cents; without a doubt you can also give me fifteen cents. Please, give me fifteen cents, that way not only can I go on the special bus, but I can also get off at the bus stop and buy two tostadas, one of guacamole and the other of salsa.* " This time I really did finish the prayer with simple but powerful words which said, just like my mother taught me, *"In the name of Jesus, amen."*

If at some point before I mentioned that my testimonies might seem like "science fiction" this will top it all off. This miracle has nothing to do with "science," it sounds like something that is just "fiction" or a tale. However it is pure reality. When I told my cousin Samuel Vargas, he told me some very interesting words, "Look, I personally don't believe anything you are telling me, but if I were to be wrong and what you are saying really did happen, **there is no doubt that God exists.** It's more, the only person who could believe this, is Aunt Minita (referring to my mother)." Said and done, my mother already knew it, I had told her. She believed me to the last detail of the wonderful story.

THREE SHINY NEW COINS ON THE GROUND IN FRONT OF ME

As soon I finished praying and saying, "In the name of Jesus, amen," I lowered my head which I had elevated to heaven, along with my gaze. In that moment the most surprising and touching wonder that has ever happened in my life occurred. When I lowered my gaze from heaven and looked at the ground, there they were. They were three, small, five cent coins, they shined like they were fresh out of the factory and had never been used (those coins are the same size as the dimes in the States). The coins were in a perfect line placed right next to each other;

it looked like a parade. When I saw them, I felt like I was going to faint and collapse to the ground. It was like a divine or angelic visitation. The miracle could not have been more palpable and real. The fright it gave me was so much so that even though I used all my strength to try and stay on my feet, it was impossible. Very slowly I bent over, lowering myself with my hands outstretched to the ground. Eventually I managed to sit down completely, meaning my buttocks were sitting on the ground itself. All this happened as I stared at the coins without touching them. They were real, they were shiny, and they were three five cent coins, which equaled fifteen cents of quetzal. It was not a fortune, but I didn't care about that, because it was exactly what I needed and, more than that, it was EXACTLY WHAT I HAD ASKED GOD FOR. There was no room for doubt; it was a miracle that God worked in favor of a 13 year old boy. Hallelujah and blessed be God's name!

The miraculous story ended after a few minutes when I recovered from the fright and decided to touch the little coins to prove they were real, and I wasn't seeing visions. My friend, I assure you they were as real as life itself. I touched them and took them in my hand. I felt like a giant hero. The God of heaven had heard me and had conceded me a miracle.   I never thought, or even cared that the sum was so small. All I cared was that God heard me in his holy heaven and answered my petition according to his riches in glory, and in honor to the faith with which I asked.

When I put the three shining coins in my hand, and then in my pocket, I felt for the first time the sensation of being a millionaire. A few meters ahead was the next bus stop. Very sure of what I had in my pocket, I stopped and waited. When I watched the filthy regular buses pass by, I felt proud, because I knew that that day I would not travel in one of them, but in a splendorous special microbus. Later the first of them arrived and with "celebrity" style I made the sign to stop. The driver's helper shouted the route, saying, "Florida, Florida, First of July, Florida, going to Florida, Foridaaaaa." He recognized that the person who stopped them was a person who had to pay double what they would for any other bus. So, not only did they stop the microbus, but when I went inside he said, "Young man, sit up front please." Wow! That was similar to "presidential treatment." In those days nobody could sit up front with the driver unless the person who shouted the route authorized it. The helper himself told me that I would go in that seat in the front row, that was similar to "First Class on American Airlines"... (ha, ha, ha, ha).

TWO CRUNCHY TORTILLAS AWAITED ME

I boarded the bus in a sector called "The Rodeo" at the Calzada San Juan Boulevard, in front of the "El Tecolote" Mall. I sat in the bus seat with all the confidence of a millionaire and **the blood in my veins was racing like a champ**. I knew that even though I only had fifteen cents, it didn't come from a common or usual place, but it came from heaven itself.

I remember it as if was today. The other passengers looked at me with admiration. I remember that not only did I get on the exclusive and desired special microbus for the middle class people, but I was chosen to be up front. I had a smile from ear to ear. I felt like I had heaven itself in my hands. I was able to enjoy the view from up front, while the other passengers traveled like well-organized sardines on a ten cent bus. I felt so good that when I descended from the bus, I directed myself in slow motion to the place where a woman was with a stack of toasted tortillas, which were cooked over a slow fire in her handmade-wood-stove (comal). With rich kid style I said, "Could you give me one of guaca and another with salsa, please?" Everything pointed to the woman noting that I had authority, because she immediately stopped what she was doing and rushed to serve me the tostadas. Incredible! With just 15 cents, I felt like I would today if I was the owner of a mansion in Newport, Rhode Island, or enjoying a day in the famed Admirals Club of American Airlines in Miami or in London Heathrow. What I asked for was served.

Please realize that although the miracle was a small provision, to me it had enormous value. What I needed in that precise moment was provided for me. To this day, I teach that "the size of the miracle does not depend on abundance, but on the need provided for."

Friend, you, who reads my manuscript and delights through "A Life of Miracles," allow me to ask you, could it be that my God is bigger than yours? Is it possible that there is a difference? Or, could it be that He is the same but He loves me more? NO WAY! There is only one God and He is ALL Powerful. He has no favorites. To God, all of his children have the same value and are loved the same. Permit me then, to motivate you in the name of Jesus to believe in your miracle today. I do not doubt at all that if you believe it today, you will receive it today. Believe my friend, and you will receive your miracle in the name of Jesus, amen.

LITTLE CARS ON MY HEAD

I had to get rid of them; they had invaded me and were destroying not only my health, but also my reputation. My physical age was about 12 years, but my spiritual age was that of a mature Christian, which is why the miracle did not wait when I declared it.

Surely you know that when a young person begins to mature, they want to act like an adult. I was becoming a man now, or at least I thought so. I liked having lots of friends, to be popular in the neighborhood and compliment the girls my age. But there was something that was affecting me, and embarrassing me... "I had little cars on my head." You may ask, what is that? That is the phrase that is used in the poor neighborhoods of Guatemala to refer to someone who has a head infested with lice. Yes, you read correctly, I had lice and nits all over my scalp. I had so many that sometimes the lice would walk along my forehead or take a stroll across my face. Forgive me if it sounds disgusting, but many times I could feel them walking and I even felt when they were having lunch on my head. I couldn't take it anymore! Even though I was very popular and I had a lot of friends, there was a neighbor (a young man) that considered me, to be his rival. I remember on one occasion, Mrs. Andrea, a woman who had a little shop around the corner from my house, shouted,

"Hello there slick (someone who is clean and good looking), you are Mrs. Mina's boy right? Such a nice boy! You're Mynor right?"

I, with a big smile, in the presence of such special praise, responded, "Yes, I am Mynor Vargas..."

Immediately the rival came up and told Mrs. Andrea in a sarcastic voice

"Yeah, this is "slick" Mynor Vargas. Just don't get close because he has a lot of little cars on his head.

When I heard that, I felt like he had thrown a bucket of cold water on my face. Full of shame, I responded, "No, you're lying…"

He didn't like that, so he launched another attack, "Let's check your head then, then we will know if it's true or not."

I COULDN'T HIDE THE SHAME

As I said, I was very popular. The people liked me, but envy consumed some. One time, we were walking in the Santa Marta Colony. We went to visit some young girls we had recently met. I quickly took initiative and started talking with one of them. One of my friends who liked her said, "Just be careful with him or you might get stuck with 'the cars'." How embarrassing! There were 25 of us in the group that day (like the little rascals gang) and right there in front of everyone, this ingrate throws a nuclear bomb at me. I had to give up my pretentions toward that girl. I realized that the girls looked at me, and smiled, but then turned their backs on me. It was as if they concentrated on my head to see if what my supposed "friends" said was true. With friends like that who needs enemies! On other occasions, the girls greeted me, and smiled at me, but they quickly glanced at my hair to verify the rumor that I had a plague of lice on my head. During that time I had a unique hair style. It was specifically designed for me by my brother-in-law Gumersindo Leon. Gumer designed two hair styles for me (the one I had in that time, and the one I have now) he did that for me for about 20 years until he retired from the profession; that it how I got this unique and original hair style.

MAMA, HOW MIRACULOUS IS GOD?

I had the fortune of always having my Papa with me, and he was a responsible and loving father. However, my mother was my confidant. One day I asked her, "Mama, how miraculous is God?" Without thinking she replied, "Why are you asking me that Mainitor (little Mynor)? What do you need God to do for you?" I explained, "Mama, you know I have lice on my head and I haven't been able to get rid of them." During that time, on my own I had tried every existing treatment to exterminate them, but nothing seemed to work and it was time to talk. I remember one time I took a bottle in my hand and pressed down, rolling it across my head to squish the invaders. If I am not mistaken, I believe I could hear when they were squashed and crushed (just remembering disgusts me). Even with that, there were no positive results. I used special, fine combs that were made to remove the eggs, and NOTHING! My mother sent me to buy a powder called "gamezan", which is a kind of lime. With a lot of love she helped me as much as she could. She diluted the gamezan in water and then poured it on my head with a plastic recipient over and over again, trying to poison the insects that had made my head their residence and my hair their mansion. Once again, there were no results. As a last resort she sent me to buy two very strong chemicals utilized to exterminate cockroaches. Their names: Baygon of Bayer's, and OKO. When I arrived home, my mother tried the first one and then the second. The plague was too dug in and wouldn't stop for anything. Weeks passed and my mother continued treating my hair, because the "blessed" lice wouldn't die. On the contrary, they got fatter and multiplied. At that point my scalp started suffering chemical burns and was very sensitive.

As a last alternative, my mother said, "Mainitor, if you want to get rid of the lice, the only solution is to take you to the barber and let him shave your head (that meant leaving me totally bald without a single hair). Almost all the children on the block suffered shavings in the recent months, but I did not want to suffer the shame. During my time shaving the head was something that only members of the army did, or those who had lice. Many of my friends, who made fun of me, also had "little cars on their head." As a matter of fact, I can assure you it was one of them who contaminated me. They had been shaved already themselves, and were totally bald.

It was at that point when I found myself with my back against the wall that I asked,

"Mama, how miraculous is God?" explaining right away that she knew I had lice.

My mother, a woman of much faith, answered me, "If you are asking because you want God to remove your lice, let me tell you that a granddaughter of the most respected elders in the Church (sister Martita and brother Matias), asked for prayer from her parents for this same reason, and God did the miracle. If you want I can call them," she added.

"NO, please don't call them Mama. Enough people already know what's happening to me. You pray with me and I'll believe for a miracle," I told her.

Mama Mina prayed for me with a lot of faith, and I asked her not to ask me about the lice for a while, since the miracle would happen. I decided to believe and only believe it would happen. I bathed every day to put my faith in works and I combed my hair the same as usual, but I didn't check, I didn't even continue applying lice killer. Every day I prayed and told God that I expected a miracle in thirty days (a key number at many times in my life). I believed that if I just prayed with faith, at the end of those days, I would be clean.

Said and done, I just prayed and waited on Jehovah. At the end of 30 days I went before the priesthood (my mother), and told her,

"Mama, I have come for you to check my head."

She took a fine comb in her hand and a white pillow case. "Did you pray Mainitor?" my mother asked.

"Yes I did," I immediately responded. "I told God that in a month I wouldn't have lice anymore," I added.

After having all my hair covered (anointed) with oil so that any larvae and lice would be dislodged, mama passed the comb through my hair the first time. Again she passed the comb a second time, and did that successively for three to five minutes using the super fine, special comb. Mama didn't say a word. I didn't either, I just had my eyes wide open to observe attentively if something of the plague were to fall on the white cloth.

THE SILENCE WAS BROKEN

The words my mother uttered were carved and saved in my memory. I can still hear the echo, the tone of voice and the amazing declaration of healing. Mama Mina told me, "It's certainly incredible Mainitor. God has done a miracle, because you don't have anything on your head." HALLELUJAH, GLORY TO GOD!

While everyone who had made fun of me had to shave their heads and suffer their own shame, I never had to do it. I cried out to God and he heard me. I remember that they continued to make fun of me even though I had been cleaned of the plague by a miracle, but that was a secret between my mother and me. They thought I was still infected. One day, at a small party in the neighborhood, they wanted to take advantage of the opportunity to humiliate me publicly. I remember how I arrived very well dressed and bathed. Some friends gave me the nickname "Outerlimits" and others "Realwest", that was due to the clothing brand I used. When I arrived at the small and humble gathering, there was music playing on the record player and various LPs on the side waiting to play all night. There were two special musical albums on the table. One of them was from the movie "Grease", which was a cinematographic success in June of the year 1978. The other was from the movie "Saturday Night Fever", which was also a box-office success in the month of November in 1977. When they saw me arrive, some of them welcomed me, saying,

"Hey guys, here comes Outerlimits."

Another said, "No, he's Realwest."

That was when one of my rivals said, "No, he is the guy with little cars on his head…"

Everyone nearby started laughing out loud. Some of them did it because they were mocking me and others did it because it just sounded too funny. I reacted very serene and surely by ignoring it. I proceeded to greet everyone cordially. That guy wanted to make me look ridiculous, so he challenged me again, saying, "If you don't have little cars on your head, let us check you right here in front of everyone."

Without a word, I went up to him and inclined my head. I put my head in front of his chest for him to examine me. My little friend was so sure he would find the plague, because he had seen before that my head was covered in lice and being that I never shaved my head, he believed he had caught me red handed. This was the moment when he was going to embarrass me in public. Everyone told him,

"There he is, right in front of you, check him…"

Neither slow nor fast, he put his hands to work. He began seeking lice as he moved my shiny and flexible hair from one side to another. He checked my hair over and over again, but there were no signs of a single larva. My shame was removed. That day I experienced the Psalm that says, *"Thou preparest a table before me in the presence of mine enemies: thou anointest my head with oil; my cup runneth over."* Ladies and gentlemen, let me tell you that not only did he check me, but half a dozen other guys did too. Right away some young girls a little older than us, came up to me and said,

"Mynor, don't let those #!@*^# (so and so), bother you anymore. I'll check you myself and if I say that what they've been saying about you is a lie, it will be declared a lie."

Those older girls checked me, and nothing. That day I was more famous than John Travolta among all those present (ha, ha, ha, ha). Apart from my charisma which has always distinguished me, many said I was a nice guy, and in that moment the whole community had confirmed that my head was clean. Forgive me for being expressive, but I can't contain myself. I have to say it again: Hallelujah, glory to God! I believe it is time for this secret to come to light. My friends will know what happened the day they read my biography. It wasn't that I never had lice; it was that God cleaned my head miraculously.

A GOLDEN CLOTH IN MY WALLET

As you will remember, at the beginning of this chapter I warned you that these little wonders might seem impossible to believe. It is here, that we will see one of the most surprising divine interventions at a specific moment.

I found myself temporarily as a missionary in Guatemala for fifteen months. The small fortune I had brought from the United States, had been totally spent. My mother gave me Q300.00 each month from rent she got for a house on her property. My brother Carlos provided the food in the elderly home "Oasis of Eden", a place that also served as a center of my operations and where I lived. I had no money, but I always had what I wanted. One day I found myself in the capital city of Guatemala beside my friend and travel assistant for Central America, Daniel Mendez. We had a craving to go eat at McDonald's. We knew very well we didn't have enough money. We started counting and together we had just a few quetzals in our pockets. Later, we were looking for all the coins we could find in my room and under the seats of my old Datsun. With what we could gather we went to the fast-food restaurant. When we arrived, a girl opened the door and told us,

"Welcome to McDonald's."

Then, the person at the counter asked, "What would you like to eat?"

With my great sense of humor, I responded,

"The question is not what we would like to eat, but what can we afford? We only have these quetzals and some coins."

She smiled at us and said, "Well, what can you afford to eat today?"

The incident was really quite funny. I opened my thin wallet and there it was... Before I could see the first green bill, I noticed threads from a golden cloth that my anonymous teacher and motivator in faith Reverend W.V. Grant Jr. had sent me. For an instant I thought, "It would sure be nice if I could exchange this cloth for a hamburger!"

That's how the "Big Little Miracle" happened. A few days before, my mail from the United States arrived. When missionaries came from the north, they did me the favor of bringing my letters and correspondence that arrived at my house in the United States.

Within all the correspondence was an envelope from the famous evangelist W.V. Grant Jr. (Walter Vinson Grant

Junior). Inside contained a long letter of about five pages full of bible quotes, messages of faith and a piece of gold colored cloth. One of the passages cited was Acts 19:11-12, *"And God wrought special miracles by the hands of Paul: So that from his body were brought unto the sick handkerchiefs or aprons, and the diseases departed from them, and the evil spirits went out of them."* Once again, I had no money, I was NOT very sought after to preach in churches that gave generous offerings. Therefore, nothing was left for me but to believe every word of faith that had a Biblical basis to sustain me. Once again I put my faith to work (nothing that is true faith can be without works, because the opposite is dead). I followed the instructions that the extensive letter said, including putting the golden cloth in my wallet. I placed it exactly where my mother told me I should keep a bill she said was for shame. "Yes children," my mother would say, "keep a bill hidden and at the moment of an emergency, you won't be ashamed, you can use it then." Right there was where I put the gold cloth, and without realizing it I had forgotten about it until that day in McDonald's. When I put it in my wallet, there was absolutely no money.

The McDonald's employee was waiting for me to order. I still hadn't asked for anything, but I had been thinking with Daniel to ask for a cheese burger for each of us from the menu, some fries and two small Coca Colas. When I opened my wallet, those golden threads called my attention. I pulled on them to get rid of them. When I did so, I pulled out what looked like American money, or dollars. My eyes have only ever opened that wide on a few occasions. I shouted really loud, saying, "Dear mother, I CAN'T BELIEVE IT!!!" Without saying anything else, I pulled out the dollars.

They were perfectly folded in two, and I discovered that there were four untouched bills of $100.00. It was $400.00 total. Daniel wanted to ask me about it, thinking I had hidden the money, and I assured him,

"NO, this is not hidden money, it's a miracle."

To all of that, the young McDonald's lady maintained a smile and asked once more,

" So, how much can you afford to eat now?"

I asked her,

"Do you accept dollars?"

She informed me that of course they did. Instead of getting a little cheese burger, we ate from an extra-large menu, including a vanilla ice cream sundae with pineapple and nuts for desert. Blessed be the name of the Lord!

When we finished eating and talking so much about miracles, Daniel Mendez told me, "Look Mynor, could it have just been chance? Maybe the money was just yours; or was it really a miracle? I explained to him that the hiding place had been checked several times before and there was nothing there. Even five days ago when I put the golden cloth there, I checked and it was empty. Therefore, there was no doubt that it was a miracle. So Daniel said to me, "Well I hope another miracle happens, because after you threw those threads on the floor, I picked them up and put them in my wallet…"

MORE THAN INCREDIBLE

I don't know how it happened, but the next day in the morning Daniel received a call from Pineda Rossell Transportation, who required him to go collect a sum of money from his brother Apolo who had sent it from the United States. Ladies and Gentlemen, a day before we had no money in our pockets, and the next day Daniel and I were on the move again in our exquisite missionary life of style. We dined in fine restaurants such as "Los Cebollines" located at the Calzada Roosevelt Boulevard and also at "The Grand Turkey Restaurant" located on that same Calzada Roosevelt Boulevard and in Zone 4 of Guatemala. That is all to say, we didn't protect those little bills like they were the last Coca Cola in the desert. We spent them on Evangelistic Tracts, and on mobilizing ourselves from one city to another, as well as eating in a big and refined way. Hallelujah, blessed be God who supplies ALL our needs, amen!

More miracles occurred with that same cloth, and in the name of Jesus. Later that year I felt I had to get rid of it, because I didn't want it to turn into an amulet. I let it go in prayer and I told the Lord, "I am letting it go because miracles don't come from a piece of gold colored cloth, but from you my God. In the name of Jesus, amen."

LAUGHTER INSTEAD OF DEATH

God is so good that many times he protects us from our own faults. I was coming from an important mission I had been on with the poor people of San Salvador, El Salvador. You might know or can imagine how the long international roads of Central America are. My travel assistant for Central America at that time, Daniel

Mendez, accompanied me once again on that journey. I was so desperate to get back to my base of operations in Guatemala, that I daringly put the car in a dangerous situation. I tried to pass a car in front of us. I estimated that if I found myself in front of a vehicle coming from the opposite direction, the driver I was passing would be kind enough to move over to the right so that all three cars could fit on the road. What I did not expect happened, the driver of the car I was trying to pass got angry because I wanted to pass him and he slammed on the gas pedal, and moved to make it hard for me to pass his vehicle. To make things worse, while both vehicles were moving at high speed beside each other on a curve, I noticed down the road another car coming toward us at a high speed as well. I instantly turned to look at the driver who did not want to let me pass asking him for mercy with my eyes and telling him to move aside. That inconsiderate and stubborn driver looked ahead and left me to the mercy of my luck.

I had a millisecond to make a decision. The possibilities were the following: 1) Ram the car beside me so that he would give me some space. 2) Wreck with the car coming from the other way. 3) Throw myself out into the abyss at my own luck. Before I could blink I made the decision: The big headed guy on the other side had no brain and it wasn't his fault, he had been born dumb and would be that way for the rest of his life. The driver in front of me was absolutely innocent, so I understood that I was the guilty one in that tight spot. So, I proceeded to yank the wheel hard to the left and my car literally went flying into the abyss, and I thought death waited for me.

MIRACLE ON THE CURB

Daniel and I felt like life was slipping through our fingers, and we screamed in unison, "ahhhhhhhhhhhhhhh!!" As we screamed, the car stopped in mid-air. It stopped completely. We couldn't believe it. We looked on both sides and it seemed like we were floating in air. We looked below and we could see the abyss. What happened? We still don't know. We just discovered that the car moved from one side to the other and we felt like we were floating in the air.

Okay, so as to not make the situation more mysterious, let me explain. We were not floating in the air, and it wasn't an angel holding the car in the heights. What had happened was that there was a very thin heap of dirt in the exact place where I threw my car off into the deep hole. Technically, a heap of dirt is a natural elevation on non-rocky terrain. So, before continuing off into the depths, the small old car got caught by the skeletal little pile of soil. All we could see was the abyss on both sides, but without a doubt there was land under the place where the car had stopped. The tires spun in the air, not one of the four were touching the ground. When we looked behind us the car of the inconsiderate driver had disappeared, the other who was going to hit us had stopped to see how we had ended up at the bottom of the cliff. When the passengers of the vehicle noticed we were there, hanging on to the weathered heap, the woman who was apparently the wife of the driver started shouting at us, "Sons of this, and sons of that." That day they reminded us of our mothers, our grandmothers and every generation before. Daniel and I barely had enough space to leave and carefully get out of the car, with the purpose of saving ourselves and asking forgiveness. Then we would justify ourselves and explain that we had made a sacrifice throwing ourselves onto the cliff so that we wouldn't crash into them. The gentleman, on the other hand, was very courteous and heard us out. That made the woman angrier, it made her shout at us and curse us with filthy and rude words. That was all we needed to start a fit of laughter. Daniel and I started to laugh until tears ran down our cheeks. It caught onto the husband, and he pointed out to us that the only person who was angry was the wife. Seeing the reaction of her husband, she insulted him as well and gave him an authoritarian order to continue on. I laughed hard and called to them, "May God bless you richly and abundantly," Hahahaha.

After that moment, when we were finally able to control our fit of laughter, some country men came and helped us get the car out and put it back on the main road.

A DATSUN OR A 4X4

I have to admit it: Our imprudence had not ended for that day. We got into the car and decided to take a short cut. We dared a steep mountain with my Little Yellow 2 door Datsun 1000. The little car was not a 4X4, it wasn't a Pick Up, it was not a big truck, it was a miniature, yellow, compact car that seemed more like a defenseless canary, or a chick. But in the rush to arrive quickly, after having been at the point of killing ourselves in the abyss, we decided to cross over the mountain. There was no asphalt there, the entire road was dirt. Sometimes we found ourselves on very steep hills, and other times we found ourselves on very pronounced descents. There were moments where the car almost flew through the air as it slid down those hills. We were witnesses of how other bigger and stronger cars got stuck on the road, but my little yellow chick continued forward.

I prayed to God, I asked for forgiveness for my crazy acts and promised never to do it again. God protected us and we arrived safe and sound, and in one piece. Of course I am referring to my friend Mendez and me, because even though the little car certainly arrived, it was not in one piece. When we opened the hood, the location of the motor, we discovered that the front was twisted and broken, the ball joints were detached and the motor was loose and separated from the mounts. Finally, the front fenders had broken off from the chassis...

I'LL BUY THE LITTLE CHICK

When we told people about our adventure and everything that happened my friends had a lot of admiration for my Datsun 1000. It was one of Tio Juan's (Uncle John) cars, he had bought it at a car junkyard in the USA. After acquiring it he serviced the motor with new spark plugs and an oil change, and finally gave it to his brother Elmer, my other uncle, so he could travel from Providence, Rhode Island to Guatemala by land. Tio Elmer arrived in Guatemala safe and sound, the next day I asked him to sell me the car. He explained to me that the automobile (if you could call it that, I called it a "method of transportation"), came from a junkyard and his brother only paid $60.00 for it. Immediately I said, "I DON'T CARE, I'll give you Q 1,500.00 (fifteen hundred quetzals) for it, all in cash." In those days, the quetzal had an exchange rate of about 3.15 per dollar. That would have meant giving him approximately $500.00 for that miraculous car. I used it all throughout my missionary trip in Guatemala. That is to say for fifteen months. When I was ready to return to the United States, my partner in missions, the evangelist Sergio Aroldo Morales Eguizabal, made me sell it to him. He told me, "Reverend, you're leaving and I want the car, so I'll buy the little chick." I reminded him of everything the car had been through, but he still insisted on buying it, and he offered me Q 6,500.00 for it. I told him, "Just give me Q 5,000.00." What do you think my dear reader? Not only did I sell it cheap, but I earned almost four times what I had paid for it. God has always been involved in my life, not just in big things, but in apparently small things as well.

UNCLE, YOU KILLED THAT BOY!

In general, I have never stayed in one place; I travel continually doing the work of God. One time, I was traveling from Zacapa to Guatemala City when, in the surrounding area of kilometer 10 on the Atlantic route, an 11 year old boy let go of his sister's hand and decided to quickly cross the road (route or small highway). When he saw my car coming at high speed, he filled with panic and froze in the middle of the road. I honked at him over and over again, at which point he tried to jump to the side. Sadly, it was too late; my car was too close and ran over him. When my nephew Pierry, who was with me, saw that I stopped after running the boy over, he said to me in English, "Let's get the hell out of here."

I asked him, "Why?"

He shouted at me, "Uncle, you killed that boy!"

I opened my door and saw that he was badly hurt, lying down lifeless. I noticed that his sister was also screaming inconsolably. I got out of the car and walked steadily, saying, "In the name of Jesus. In the name of Jesus." I repeated that phrase dozens of times.

His sister appeared and started punching me, hitting me everywhere, screaming at me, "You killed my brother!"

I continued walking. I don't remember any of the punches hurting me, but I didn't even slow down. Steadily I walked toward the child like I was hypnotized or in a trance. When I arrived at the place where the child was laying, I took him in my arms. He was so big that it was hard for me to pick him up, but without anyone's help I did. I said out loud, "In the name of Jesus." I never asked for anything, I didn't say a specific prayer, I just begged with unspeakable groaning and in Spanish I said, "En el nombre de Jesús" (In the name of Jesus). With the child in my arms and uttering over and over the name that is above every name, I twisted halfway, turned partially, and then started making full turns, looking at the curious crowd that had gathered while I continued saying "In the name of Jesus".

I could hear them saying, "He killed him."

Others said, "He ran over him!"

I continued for approximately two minutes with the young man in my arms while I received punches from the older sister. I never stopped saying out loud, "In the name of Jesus." All of a sudden the child groaned, opened his eyes, came to himself and stretching out, stood on the ground. Then he asked, "What happened to me?"

Right away the sister told him, "This man was going to kill you."

I instantly corrected her and said, "What happened is that God just revived you…"

WITHOUT REALIZING IT,
I WAS A CELEBRITY

In about ten minutes, not only were there hundreds of people at the scene of the accident, but an ambulance from the Volunteer Fire Department arrived. When they saw the child walking, they couldn't believe it. They decided to take him to the hospital to examine him. When they asked me my name, I answered, "Mynor Vargas," and it turned out that all the firemen listened to my radio program "A Fragment of Hope," for which, with admiration they asked me,

"Are you the radio evangelist?"

"That's right," I responded.

"Then don't worry, we have to go cover another accident, take him to the hospital yourself so they can examine him, because if we take him you will be arrested immediately."

The curious people around me said,

"Brother Mynor, take him yourself, so that the police won't arrest you." To my surprise, everyone knew me. I was in total agreement with them; I didn't want to sleep in jail even for a single night. The firemen were leaving when the National Police patrol arrived.

They started taking the respective information and when they heard my name was Mynor Vargas, the commanding officer who was far away asked,

"Aren't you the famous radio preacher?"

I quickly responded,

"In reality, I'm not famous, but yes, I am Mynor Vargas from *A Fragment of Hope*."

The officer told me,

"You talk to the family, because if we make a report, we'll have to arrest you."

Without saying much more, the police disappeared from the scene. The mother of the child arrived at the scene and asked me, "Who are you? Why did the firemen and police leave?"

I answered her, "Ma'am, my name is Mynor Vargas."

She looked at me firmly with surprise, almost in disbelief. Later she told me, "I listen to Radio VEA (Evangelic Voice of America) and you are my favorite preacher. Don't worry about it; let's just take my son to the doctor so they can examine him."

Things definitely don't happen by chance. A week before I had met with my old time friend, Doctor Leslie Johnson, who had given me his phone number. I remembered how he told me, "If you have any emergencies, here is my business card." Right then I called him, and it turned out he lived close to the scene of the accident and we drove to his house.

Being there, Dr. Johnson told us, "This child has nothing more than some minor scrapes on his elbow and one on his head. It looks like he fell off a bike, not like a car ran over him."

The mother was in agreement that we would leave the matter at that. I offered her an offering in case the child wanted something and I gave her my business card in case there was any need for surgery in the future. She told me,

"God has done a miracle, he won't need anything else."

HE ALMOST CUT MY HEAD OFF

When I arrived to leave them at the road where the accident occurred, it was already night. Without knowing it there was a man hiding on the bushes waiting to kill me. He came out all of a sudden with a giant machete, ready to cut off my head. In reality, he had a guarizama (a really long, curved machete, used for agricultural work). As I asked him to let me explain, he responded,

"No, you son of a....," he swung the machete over and over at my head. Fortunately, I had very good reflexes while he was attacking.

I spoke again, "Sir, your son is alive by a miracle, let me explain."

However, the man continued insulting me, and wanting to decapitate me. The wife jumped in between us and grabbed him by his collar to tell him in his ear, "He is Brother Mynor Vargas."

"Ahhh! What did you say?"

So she repeated again out loud, "He is Brother Mynor Vargas from *A Fragment of Hope*."

The man went pale and silent. He took the machete and threw it far into the bushes. He immediately asked me to forgive him, at the same time kneeling in front of me. I told him not to worry about it, that his attitude to defend his son was normal, but to please not try to kill anyone else, because he was a Christian. That father was so embarrassed, that when he realized I was giving the offering I had promised to the mother, he didn't want to receive it. I insisted, and gave them the offering and my business card to take responsibility for everything.

He said, "Okay then, but only because you insist, but all I know is that God did a miracle." Without going back into the subject, the man and his family walked down the road and disappeared. To this day it has not been necessary for them to communicate with me. My nephew Pierry and I were left with our mouths wide open at everything that happened that day, and still today, twenty years later, the shock has not left us. Our All Powerful God freed us from the worst and turned it into a giant miracle. Hallelujah, amen!

7

THE MIRACLE OF LIVING LIKE A MILLIONAIRE, WITHOUT BEING A MILLIONAIRE

"A friend of his took him in a luxurious car, to that international airport from where he would take his transatlantic flight. The traveler went elegantly dressed with his fine brand name suit made by Oscar de la Renta, and colorful tie. As soon as he entered the terminal, an assistant accompanied him the whole way, carrying his bags to the counter. Immediately the distinguished world traveler gave him a generous tip. He avoided the long line to check his baggage, because he was standing at the counter for first class travelers. The attention they gave him was exclusive. His bags were set apart from the others with a special orange colored tape that said "Priority Passenger." While he waited for the plane to leave, he lounged comfortably in the "Admiral's Club." He was among the first passengers to board the Boeing 777-200. He sat in his comfortable and ample leather seat which could turn into a bed with the touch of one of the 18 different position buttons. A few minutes later, the plane took off. As soon as the takeoff phase was finished, the stewardess, who he had asked to take his jacket, brought him a cup of black coffee. Later, they gave him a menu for him to choose his favorite meal and some wine for good digestion. The trip was comfortable, so our traveler took out his iPod and during the journey he listened to his favorite music as he enjoyed a flavorful desert. Later, he opened his leather briefcase and took out his laptop. He was going to take advantage of the time to work on one of the conferences that he would be speaking about at his destination. As soon as he arrived, he was taken in an executive vehicle to the 5-star hotel where he would stay. His suite was already reserved. It had a large room with a king size bed. Aside from that it had a living room, with a desk and high speed internet connection, a dining area and an enormous marble bathroom, equipped with pressurized shower head for warm water massages which could also be used to fill the huge Jacuzzi. Three hours after arriving, he met with the event organizer, who confirmed that he was the Official Conference Speaker at the International Congress. The host took him to a sumptuous restaurant. The location gave a nice impression. It was a friendly place with small rooms that offered certain privacy. The menu provided a variety of entrees, salads, soups, main plates, drinks and deserts. The attention was first class. The waiters were educated and attentively served the man who would be the best tipper of the moment. They were in the perfect environment to refine the last details of the massive event. The next day, the multitude of people listened with much attention and excitement to the powerful Biblical message our protagonist offered."

Although you may not believe it, my dear reader, that fiery gentleman and International Conference speaker who was described in the story above, is me. But please, don't be mistaken, I am not a millionaire, even though in many stages of my life, I've lived as if I were one. Let me say it again, "**I am not a millionaire!**" I live with my wife, my children and my pets, in a three story house I am still paying off to the bank. I drive a Ford Expedition from the year 2003 that my brother gave me, my wife has a Mercedes Benz C230 from the year 1997, which was practically a gift. So both cars were given to us. Those are all of our belongings. I assure you that if you added the value of all my belongings and the few dollars I have in my bank account, the sum would be far from the first million dollars.

However, I have had the privilege of traveling to 4 continents and more than 27 countries in the world. Some of them I have been to 5, 10, or more times. I am in love with our blue planet, which is 71% covered in water and has only 29% of firm land. I have flown more than two million miles on American Airlines alone, aside from the hundreds of miles on other airlines. Being that the earth has a diameter of 12,756 kilometers, I have gone about 250 times around the globe (I doubt if even Superman has done that…). As you read at the beginning of this chapter, I always travel first class and generally I stay at 5 star hotels and resorts or luxury villas. I certainly like to know and enjoy the beautiful planet where God has put us; its mountains, oceans, rivers and lakes, and its picturesque villages as well as its modern cities. **But above all, I love the people** and they are my main motive for traveling and preaching the message of Salvation by grace through Jesus Christ. I know perfectly well that our Lord Jesus died for everyone in the world we live in, and that currently there is close to seven billion people. More than four billion are not Christians.

For that reason I am a pastor in a local church in the city of Providence, Rhode Island, United States of North America. At times I have been the Senior Pastor of three churches located in three different cities at the same time, preaching and ministering up to 8 times during a weekend. A car waiting for me as I finish one sermon, to take me right away to the next church where, upon entering, I go directly to the pulpit ready to preach again. For that same reason, I am the founder of the Shalom International Church Consortium which has more than 600 affiliated churches around the world. That is why I instituted and direct the International Federation of Christian Chaplains, Inc. with more than 1,800 subordinate affiliates in 40 countries, for whom I am in charge of as General Commander. With that in mind, I founded my own Christian University named "Crown Theological Seminary of New England." Because of the burden I carry within me, we at the Continental Radio Network produce four different radio programs which have transmitted in 922 radio stations, 10,000 programs a month and are heard by approximately 12,000,000 listeners. This is why I currently travel up to 100,000 miles each year all over Latin America, the Caribbean, parts of Europe and Asia, to continue expanding the Kingdom of God on this earth. Again I repeat, **I am not a millionaire**, but the Lord in his sovereign will has given me the privilege of **living like a millionaire**. I did not achieve that because I ask for a determined amount of money as fees and offerings for my participation on Christian events. It is simply the grace of God poured out on the life of this servant who he took out of misery and has freed from premature death on multiple occasions.

I GIVE LIKE A MILLIONAIRE

Some or many parts of my book will seem to you like fantasy or science fiction, like a fairy tale, but the truth is all to the contrary. This is my life, it is my reality, and it is my daily living. I am the best tipper on almost every occasion; there is nobody like me, your servant, who gives such generous tips. I say nobody, until my two brothers Salvador and Carlos arrive. They are the champions of the world in that aspect. While in Latin America the custom is the give a 10% tip, I give 15, 20, and up to 30%. My brothers on the other hand, give up to 300%. In the United States the official tip is between 15 and 18%, I give 20 to 30% as a minimum. For me the subject of compensation is not just giving when you have to give, but to give everywhere. To the person who opens the door for me to enter a hotel, to the person who carries my bag, who brings me an iron, who brings me an extra towel, who prepares my table or gives me a smile. To all of them the same, I give a tip. My close friends will not let me lie; they know that I am a crazy giver. In case you have forgotten, I have to remind you again, **I am not a millionaire**, and I only give according to what I receive. Of course, there are people who don't open the door for me; they haven't even done me a favor. To the contrary, they have treated me badly, they have criticized me, they have marginalized and slandered me. However, even to them I give tips in cold hard cash. That is who I am and that is my life, the life of a millionaire, without necessarily being one.

While I have never managed to accumulate a large sum of money in savings, the money has never run out. It seems like a mystery, the more I give, the more it flows. What a mystery! No? I call it a miracle. My friends have difficulty believing me and I have had to prove that I have no money in the bank. Many of them assure that

I have thousands of dollars hidden somewhere or saved in different bank accounts, while my brothers and closest family have been convinced that I have nothing, nothing, NOTHING! Well, in reality I do have a bank account, and the only reason I have it is to get rid of the zero. The current balance I have accumulated is $23.04. That isn't even enough for dinner at a restaurant.

I KNOW HOW TO HONOR MINISTERS OF GOD

When it comes to attending to great Patriarchs or Ministers of God, I don't know if anyone beats us. My family and I have hosted some of the biggest preachers (meaning, of great ministerial reach) and Christian worship singers in the world. We have given them the best love offerings. It fascinates me to see the faces of the Ministers of God who have traveled the mountains on a donkey or in a truck, when on our behalf there is a limousine waiting for them, an executive helicopter or a small private plane. The same happens when they arrive at a suite, mini-suite or master suite in the best hotels. They eat in first class restaurants and, why not say it; they receive from us the best love offerings in the entire continent. My brothers and I have been able to hear over and over again the most distinguished preachers in Latin America express to us and confess that the offering we gave was the biggest they had ever received. The glory be to God; he permits us to give like millionaires without actually being millionaires. I prefer to live like a millionaire without being one, than be one without living like it... Who could have imagined that a poor family from the mountains and shacks would be champions in giving and donating love offerings, giving left and right?

MY FAMILY IS A MIRACLE

My history of miracles would be incomplete if I did not give reference to my brothers and sisters, and my nephews and nieces. To all of us, God has given the gift of traveling and enjoying the earth and creation. I know families where one or two have the pleasure of vacationing or going once in a while to a restaurant. We, without being millionaires, always eat at fine restaurants and we ALL travel continuously; although, without wanting to boast, I am still the one who flies the most. At the age of 26 days, my youngest son Matthew was already traveling with me to a massive crusade in Central America.

On the other hand, Lety, my youngest sister and her husband Alfonso Lima, have been fearless fighters and entrepreneurs. They are faithful tithers and in that way give left and right. There is no doubt that Lety and Alfonso have the house they possess by pure miracle of God. It is a double mansion with many acres of open land for horses, ponies, cows, sheep, chicken, ducks, peacocks, etc. That is not mentioning the gigantic garage for 5 cars, along with a gymnasium and a private school inside the complex. They are not millionaires either, but they are brave Christians who move by faith and take advantage of every opportunity in their path. It's not bad to have a younger sister like this, right? It's more amazing coming from a family that was born into a family sealed into extreme poverty. We have not acquired all of this because we are more intelligent than anyone else, but because the favor of God is on us.

My sister Magda, married to Gumersindo Leon, and Trinis married to Waldemar Rosales (whom I have mentioned earlier), both have two houses each. Their children are Christians and they live lacking nothing.

Both are faithful tithers and contribute to good causes. They constantly travel. Magda went on vacation 4 times last year (2009). My sister Trinis will go two weeks after the day I finish writing this chapter, on a second cruise through the Caribbean. Trinis is a professional in sociology and psychology, a career she studied as an adult. Being that, Magda is a housewife and even without working in recent years, she lives with all her commodities.

My brother Salvador, on his part, is married to Amelia. He is the founder of the church I pastor. When he retired, he called me so that I would take the church and left me directing it without any conditions. Also, he sold me the house I have now and years later he gave me two cars, a Cadillac Seville and a brand new Ford Excursion. Salvador knows the meaning of living off miracles. Multiple times he has experienced a shower of money from heaven. He has enjoyed some of the best contracts of custom jewelry and work as a contractor, etc. He has always been well paid and in one day he has made enough money to equal that of a year's salary. To this day Salvador does not have a bank account or money accumulated. Salvador has a nice house with 41 acres of land in the state of Rhode Island. His little farm to him is like a hobby. He has 35 cows and some bulls, a lot of goats, chickens and three dogs. Also, he owns a recreation center in Guatemala with its own river where emerald colored water flows. The churches use that same place for spiritual retreats or to do short term missionary projects. He recently sold another recreation center with four big pools, slides, ranches and much more, called "Las Hamacas" (The Hammocks). He has already given away or spent all of that money.

My brother Carlos is the oldest of the men and is married to Cheryl (North American). He is a strong man when it comes to the advance of the ministries, and fund raising and donations. The complex where his diverse ministries have been founded has expanded to more than 3,000 acres of land. In that place, there are 300 people working full time and at times there are up to double that amount of employees. The staff comes from humble country people to teachers, architects and lawyers and business administration professionals, etc. They all earn first class wages. You can go personally, interview any of the employees and nobody with proof could tell you that it is a scant salary. We believe that people should be well paid. **We "do not live from the poor, but we live for the poor."** We live to provide them with opportunities for a better life, starting with the immediate opportunities that we can offer. Carlos's ministry currently gives food to hundreds of thousands of homeless children and elders. Aside from that, my two brothers prepare big meetings for 300, 400, 500 and more pastors. All come without him charging a single cent and listen to the most important conference speakers, evangelists and preachers on the continent. And if that wasn't enough, he gives each participant minister an exquisite lunch beside huge pools belonging to the ministry and also vouchers to redeem free merchandise from the ministry stores. We never charge to come for any event. Carlos is recognized one of the people who offers the most help in our country, his ministry imports 500 industrial containers with donations to Guatemala through "Hope of Life." He also appears on the list of one of the 100 most influential people in Guatemala in a text book that is used in the public schools, together with several presidents, athletes, singers, etc.

All of my nieces and nephews are Christians, there isn't a single unbeliever. Some are very devoted and congregate each week in church. They worship in the services, they listen to the messages, and they are magnificent in giving offerings and faithful tithers. I have some nephews who

are believers, but DO NOT go to church every Sunday
and have stopped their offerings and tithing (they lose
the blessings, however God brings them one way or
another...). They go occasionally on special days to the
church. However, they believe in Jesus, they gave him
their lives to be saved, they pray, occasionally they give
offerings and they do good works. I pray fervently for
them and even fast, so that more than just knowing Jesus,
they may have an intimate relationship with Him. The
miracle will happen sooner than we think.

My children are not perfect (no individual is), but they
are excellent people. They are all born again Christians.
They all go to church, they all worship, they all listen to
the sermons, and they all pray. From the smallest to the
biggest they know how to be generous and fulfill what
the Bible says about the tithe and the offering. I have
five beautiful seedlings: Mynor Gabriel (Gabe), he is the
oldest at 26 years old. He is a fighter and a brilliant boy.
It doesn't matter the situation that is presented, he will
always overcome it. Lately he has been asking me a lot
about ministry. Mark Andrews is the next; he is 23 years
old and helps me in ministry, especially in the preparation
of the University I bought. He is married to Lluvia and has
a handsome baby named Andres who is only four months
old (Little Andres, my second grandchild). Sheyna is the
only girl among the four boys; she is 20 years old and is
my executive assistant in the International Ministries and
my future "Executive Vice President." Jacob Timothy is
18 years old. He is very intelligent and since he was a
little boy he has been fascinated with making money. My
brother Carlos gave him all the equipment to start a small
gardening and landscaping business. Jacob is the father of
my first grandchild, Gabriela Alexandra who is 2. Finally
my young last one is Matthew who is 13 years old. He says
he will be the one left pastoring the church. He has said it

in public and from the altar. Matthew lives and walks by my side the majority of the time. He accompanies me 3 to 4 hours before starting the church services. He studies in a private Christian school and says he does it because he is going to be the Pastor of Shalom. Matthew is very noble, and of course in his genes run the desire for the good life.

I cannot forget to mention my beloved Blanuzkia, the woman God put in my path to love her and be loved by her. Blanqui and I met at the age of 14 and 15 respectively, I being the older. We were friends for approximately five months and then we became boyfriend and girlfriend for the next year and a half. When we were married nobody had faith that the marriage would work... We were so young that it seemed like a delusion or insanity. When we asked permission from the State of Rhode Island for a marriage certificate, they sent us to Court. The lawyers of the State, the Family Counselors and the Judge could not contend with the answers I gave to each one of their questions. The Judge told me, "I am going to give you permission, but only because I don't have any argument to refute your answers, and because of your excellent work record, even though you are so young, and because of your good conduct. But because of your age there is not any assurance that this marriage is going to work." The situation is that now we have been happily married for 29 years. I must confess I don't love Blanqui the same, I LOVE HER MUCH MORE! She is my ideal partner and even though she isn't involved 100% in the ministries, she is dedicated to being the woman who makes me happy. Blanqui is not given to extravagance (in that she is different than me). She likes simple things without much detail. On my side, I am drawn to the big, the excellence and details in singular things, etc. However Blanqui very much enjoys watching me with my styles and particular characteristics. She knows that I give a nickname to everything, from pets, to cars, to my house, etc. It seems like she has fun observing who I am and loving me as that, without limits. For that reason I could not leave out of my biography, "A Life of Miracles," a special mention of her. Blanqui is my love and is my life. We live a real and unending romance. I desire my esteemed readers and friends, that this will also be the reality in your life and marriage.

My family is beautiful, and with that declaration I don't want to say that we are perfect, not even close to it. In my family we have faced adverse situations, but nothing more than normal. When the Vargas's have faced unfavorable situations, the first thing we do is get together and recognize our limitations, and pray to God so he will help us. It is a wonder to recognize that in each unfavorable circumstance, after praying, the hostility disappears and once again we are more than conquerors in Christ Jesus. With this affirmation I leave it clear that we are what we are by divine grace and not because we are intellectuals or because we deserve it. For many decades in my family there was not a single university graduate. On the contrary, we all dropped out in elementary school. Magda, Carlos and Salvador only got to second grade in elementary school. Trinis to fifth, Lety to third, and I legally only graduated from the first grade of elementary school... I will clarify that I was in third grade for six months, three days in fourth grade and a year in fifth. They were North American schools and up to this day I don't know why they didn't let me stay in any of the classes. I also don't remember ever seeing a certificate for being outstanding. When I became an adult I studied by correspondence and distance, and in my office I treasure some 20 diplomas or more. Those include six doctorates, two Doctor of Divinity Degrees, one Doctor in Theology, another Doctorate in Ministry, a Doctorate in Religious Education and finally a Doctor of Philosophy in Ministry (Ph.D.). Somehow it makes me think a lot because universities continue to call me to confer to me Honorary Doctorate Degrees or "Life Experience Degrees" in diverse specialties which I have never studied sufficiently. But if they come on God's behalf, if they are institutions of reputation and they do it in honor of the work I have done, then I will follow up and accept them. One day, I will present my collection of doctorates like a Picasso paint exposition (ha, ha, ha, ha). The reason why I say all of this is because I also consider it to be a rather unusual miracle. What's more, I myself don't know anybody who has so many doctorates coming from distinguished universities, without having passed at least half their lives studying in schools, private academies and even monasteries, etc. My case is very exceptional since almost my entire life I have passed in the practice of ministry.

Being that I am how I am and this is my biography, I have to pull out EVERYTHING about EVERYTHING that is around me. So here comes a brief story about my famous and beloved pets. I am the master and owner of several dogs and a cat. They are all legally registered and have my last name Vargas; that is very common in the United States. My first pet, in my adult age, I acquired 13 years ago. It is my Basset Hound named "Floppy." She as well as my other pets, appears in my mini-biographies, on my web page and in my international conferences. Floppy arrived at my house on a nice and white Christmas day in the year 1997. She was a collective gift that my wife and I gave to our children. She has been part of our family ever since. Just two days ago (I write this in July of 2009), because of her old age, she passed away (remember that 13 in dog years is the equivalent of 91 human years). My dog Floppy is buried in my garden at the "Cliff House."

After that is my Basset Hound "Nacho," who believes he is the king and owner of everything. My other dogs don't eat until he has filled himself with plenty of food and water. Nacho is 7 and was a gift to me. As I write, my wife is taking him for a walk because he has passed the last three days and part of the night howling because of Floppy. In third place is the Basset Hound "Pebbles," she is the youngest of the Bassets and is 5 years old. I got her at a canine farm and she is pure bred. Getting to the end of my pets is "Juicy", who is my little Mini Pincher. Because she is so small, she lives inside the house. Mini Pinchers believe they are Dobermans and are always on the defense and barking whenever a stranger walks in front of the house. Next is my other Mini Pincher "Coco," who died about a year ago, after being hit by a car. He escaped from the house to go on an adventure and that's where the accident happened. Coco is buried at the other end of my flower garden with the flowers I bought in Holland. I could not stop without mentioning my new pet, a red furred Chihuahua named "Chavela." I don't know why, but I always forget her name and end up calling her "Chalupa," but she doesn't care. The interesting thing is that she adopted me as her master… In reality she belongs to Mark and Lluvia, but she passes the days sitting by my side in the office. During my last nine day trip to the mountains of Guatemala, she sat in my chair and didn't move until I came back. She has been my companion in the majority of my time writing this book and has really won my heart. Well, the list ends with my cat "Tiger Armani." Since she arrived at the house, I taught her to be strong and that's why she thinks she is a true tiger… You won't believe me, but when she walks, she takes three steps forward, looks both ways serenely, and then takes a few more steps. In that way she has her own style. She goes out to hunt in the mornings and when her prey is in position to be attacked, she jumps as high as 5 or 6 feet to trap them. When we all watch television, she arrives with her fiery spirit and then sets herself on the backrest of the couch, as if she was the owner of the house. I think I have ministered a lot of optimism to my pets.

A LITTLE BIT MORE ABOUT FIRST CLASS TRAVEL

When I go on airplanes I tell my brothers or companions, that the poor are going in first class and the rich in coach. On multiple occasions I have upgraded great preachers, celebrity International speakers, famous artists, business men, politicians and millionaires who fly economy class, to first class. I consider all of that to be a miracle, because it should be the opposite don't you think?

I acknowledge that I like fine things and also enjoy living a good life, however I confess that I don't seek it, it just comes to me. This is so much the case, that many times when I rent a car, I arrive at the counter and they tell me, "Mr. Vargas, we are sorry but the compact car you solicited is not available. However, we will give you a Diamond Mitsubishi or a Lincoln Continental." The same thing has happened in hotels where as a joke I tell whoever is the receptionist attending me, "Could you give me a suite with an ocean view at the price of a regular room please?" and before I know it I find myself right there, in a suite with an ocean view and I paid the minimum. Glory to God for that! Many only dream of that, I think that some don't have it because they are so allergic to good things, that to the extreme they criticize those who take vacations, and travel in good cars and have nice houses. As Christians and children of the King of kings and Lord of lords, we should live well and desire the best. Please note that I said, "Desire" not "ambition." That gives testimony that we are part of the Kingdom of God.

For all the enjoyed luxuries I have shared, I almost never pay for any of them. Someone else will pay, usually the people who invite me to an event or vacation. For example, American Airlines gives me all upgrades to first class. They do it because I am a loyal traveler on their airline. They distinguish me as a "Platinum Executive" traveler each year and "Platinum for Life." Just thinking about where I could get all the money for upgrades scares me! The same thing happens with everything else. For example, at restaurants many times my friends pay for them and other times I pay. I have experienced the owner of the restaurant himself take the bill and pay for it out of his own pocket. It's worth saying that when I do pay, I do it with the same money someone else has given me.

I HAVE LEARNED
TO INVITE OTHERS

When I was only 24 years old, I organized the first Congress of Christian Communicators and Radio Broadcasters "CERCC 89." At age 26, I structured the second of the same kind. In "CERCC 89" 154 Ministers of Mass Media from 5 countries assisted. In "CERCC 91", the attendance was made up of 356 Ministers of Radio, Television, and the Press from 9 countries. These events were one of a kind; I did not charge a single cent to anyone. I donated everything, including a meal in the ballroom located in the last level of that hotel; it was a huge banquet for all the pastors. For me it was a dream come true and in reality I felt very joyful, satisfied and proud to be a "Man of Miracles." It is normal for a millionaire to pay for and invite hundreds of people to a gala lunch or dinner, but a poor boy coming from the mountains...hmmmm..., that does not sound so obvious. It sounds more like "A Miracle." These great events took place at the famous Ritz Continental Hotel in the capital city of Guatemala. The financial limitation never overshadowed the excellence of our events. They could have ended up being in the room of some church, or in a cafeteria or pantry, etc., but excellence, distinction and delicacy form part of the calling of God on the ministry I direct. Therefore, it was almost a divine demand; at least I consider it to be that way.

TODAY FOR YOU, TOMORROW FOR ME

I am in no way a parasite or freeloader. Let me explain since I have already shared that others almost always pay for me. What really happens is that I reap what I have sowed and I continue sowing it. Galatians 6:7 clearly points out, *"Be not deceived; God is not mocked: for whatsoever a man soweth, that shall he also reap."* I unendingly give left and right and in the same way I continuously receive gifts from those I least imagine would give them. That is to say, I am not a pond; I am a river through which resources flow. I could not count and even try to calculate the hundreds of people I have invited to eat at restaurants. On occasions when I participate in an International Congress, I go to a restaurant to eat and I see tables close to me with people I know. So I call the waiters and I ask them for the bills of all the people at the other tables, I pay, and I disappear; that way I avoid being thanked by the person. My Brothers do the same thing but on a much bigger scale. The fun thing is that as I am sowing I already begin reaping. Not long ago I found myself in a very fine restaurant in Sierra de las Minas,

Guatemala. An elegant gentleman greeted me from another table, waving his hand. I didn't recognize him, but regardless I stood up and I gave a very gallant salute. The surprising thing was that the gentleman, before he left, paid my bill. I saw that he was traveling in an armored car and was surrounded by bodyguards, because the waiter arrived and told me the elegant man had paid for me and left me the following message, "God bless you, Brother Mynor." Later I realized the man was not a Christian, but he used to listen to me preach when I arrived in those regions. What strange things occur in my life! I don't say that out of resentment, but because it is reality. In my case, on very rare occasions have evangelical pastors invited me to eat. However non-believers, like good business people and others who are on a bad road, have paid for my bill. I think that it is time for ministers of God to learn to be generous in inviting others out. We should be good examples. If you are stingy, don't hope to reap anything other than misery; but if you are a giver, you will receive the fruit of the seed you plant in others (*"But this I say, He which soweth sparingly shall reap also sparingly; and he which soweth bountifully shall reap also bountifully"* 2 Corinthians 9:6).

FROM THE JUNGLE TO SKYSCRAPERS

Not long ago I was invited to a dinner at a luxurious restaurant called "The Signature Room at the 95th." This place was located on the 95th level of the "John Hancock Center" skyscraper in Chicago, Illinois. The motive for going was to share a time of Christian fellowship with the famous multimillionaire baseball player Carlos Zambrano. The seafood was exquisite, but what I enjoyed more was looking out the glass walls at the great city. Over and over again the following came to my mind, "I come from the jungle and now I'm in the heights." Could there be someone who really knows who I am? I knew, and I will always know who Mynor Vargas is. I am "A Walking Miracle" by the power of God. I am someone who was born on a humble bit of a ranch.

MY FAMILY PARTIES

Some who know me say that andropause has affected my common sense, because we have the best family parties, as splendid as they can be; I have achieved parties like a magnate. Only a rich person can throw a party like I do, that is if the person feels like doing it that way, since there may be an overflow of money; but not much interest. For me money is not overflowing nor lacking, it simply appears and I put it to work in good ways. Others say I should spend the money in another way or more wisely. I tell them that each one has the right to spend their own money how they consider best. I will continue spending and investing mine in the way God guides me and I will try to be a good steward of the resources he puts in my hands. I will give to the poor, I will share with my family and I will especially invest in the expansion of the Kingdom of God here on earth, preaching the Gospel of salvation by grace through Jesus Christ. I clarify this because I don't think its right for someone to tell me what to do with what is mine. In that sense, each person is responsible before God. On my part, I make sure not to sin against my God and not step on anyone in my path and later I do what I think is best with what is mine, PERIOD!

After such a broad clarification, I will tell you about my family parties. I love my family and nobody is more important in my life than my brothers and sisters, and my beautiful nieces and nephews (In Spanish I call them "Sobrinizkios"). I am very close to all of them. I love my brothers and sisters. I live for them and I celebrate their lives. I have a lot of friends, and they are part of my life too. One of my favorite songs since I was a boy is by the Brazilian singer Roberto Carlos, "I want to have a million friends." When I have a party for friends, I invite everyone I can pay for. In the case of family reunions, they are exclusively for my family.

I will tell you of my parties according to "Mynor Vargas Creations." Up to the day I was married, nobody in the Hispanic community of Rhode Island had ever celebrated a wedding in a hotel. I contracted the Ramada Inn in Seekonk, Massachusetts and invited all the people I knew. **I left no one out of the guest list**. I was only 17 years old and I paid for the whole event with my own money which I earned working at "Mohawk Metals Recycling." The food, the lights, the tuxedos or penguin style suits, everything was first class. That is to say, I didn't limit myself, I actually went into excess. Two decades and a half later, for my 25th wedding anniversary, I rented the famous yacht "Odyssey One of Boston." That is a luxury vessel for 600 people. There I accommodated 77 members of my closest circle. They were my family and intimate associates. That night we partied like never before. We celebrated 25 years of a successful marriage with my beloved Blanuzkia (that is my nickname for my wife Blanca). I wanted to take half the world and fill the boat with 600 friends, but there wasn't enough money. That night was unforgettable. We navigated through the Boston bay at approximately 22 knots per hour. The lights from the skyscrapers illuminated the water on that night with a full moon. My family and closest friends were with us. The food and music were select. Everything was of glamor and exuberance which was apparently undeserved.

Please realize that this was the 25th wedding anniversary of a boy who came from the mountains and not of some mogul, monarch or what they call in the United States a "Tycoon." It wasn't any of them. It was the anniversary party of a country boy refined by force, who was living a life of miracles for the glory of God.

Twenty six of us were transported by a super limousine, the biggest in the States of Rhode Island and Massachusetts with a capacity for 26 people; the same one baseball players and executives of Fortune 500 businesses use. When it was all over, Blanqui and I went on a first class transatlantic trip on American Airlines to Osaka, Japan, where a modern, luxurious and romantic castle awaited us. It was "The Great Otani" located in the city of Shiromi Chuo-ku, Osaka. You tell me, doesn't it sound like I am talking about some other person and not the son of a poor countryman, or the filthy boy they wouldn't open the door for? It sounds to me like a story of someone belonging to royalty in one of those countries that have marquees. Although truthfully, I do form part of royalty. The apostle Peter tells us the following, *"But ye are a chosen generation, a royal priesthood, an holy nation, a peculiar people; that ye should shew forth the praises of him who hath called you out of darkness into his marvelous light"* (1 Peter 2:9). Therefore, every born again Christian is part of the royal family of God and should desire the best. I repeat, "Desire" not "ambition."

I HOPE TO NOT OFFEND ANYONE

With this whole story, I hope nobody gets aggravated. It is about being crystalline as suggested to me by my best mentor Dr. Paul Edwin Finkenbinder; crystalline, that is how people know me. I ask God, that no reader will get the wrong idea; that I tell these things with arrogance or ostentation. No my dear friend, in no way, I do it only to exalt the name of our God. He is the one who does everything in my life. I never spend my money in greed. I only live with what I have in front of me. As long as comfort is in my path, I will walk on it, because I am not allergic to anything of excellence.

TRINIS'S FIFTIETH

As you know, there are some things that have no repair, while other things do. Because of the fact that my sister Trinis was born right on the 24th of December, the date Christmas is celebrated in Latin America, she never had the joy of getting birthday presents. It can't even be said that there were parties for her on the anniversary of her life. One time I heard her say, "Nobody has ever celebrated my birthday…" That was enough to put into my mind and heart the desire that the day I had enough money, I would throw the party of the year for my beloved sister. It turned out that the day never arrived when I had enough money, I continue being the person who can't sustain much money, but what I do have is "much faith" and "much courage." When it came close to her 50th birthday I spoke with my brothers and sisters. I sent an email to my nephews and nieces and organized the biggest birthday party the Vargas family has had it its entire history.

A SINGLE PARTY, BUT BIG

She could not have wanted a better party. After everything, Trinis had her first birthday party, but it was the best of them all. The cost went into thousands of dollars. My brother Carlos provided 25% of the cost. A little more I collected from other family members who were able to contribute. The majority of the percentage of the cost, I put in. What a privilege to be able to pay so much money for my extremely beloved sister Trinis! I give glory to God for the honor of being the greatest contributor to that party. This is a luxury my beloved reader, a luxury that no person born in the mountains can give and not believe in miracles. Each and every one of those invited passed through a thousand wonders that night. The entire family came, a total of 78 people. Once again I would have liked to have had everyone there, but finances and other factors did not permit it. So it was just closest family present on that occasion. The exception was two couples of friends, Jaime Najera with his wife Evelyn, Mainor Aldana with his wife Olga and Andrea, their daughter. Annette Peterson also participated, the person who helped my sister Trinis arrive to the United States.

Why was the celebration so costly? I will give you some of the main reasons: 1) because the food was served by the professional catering business called "My Home Restaurant." 2) Because professional videographer and cameraman were contracted for the entire night. 3) Because there was constant music by a DJ from Massachusetts and live Mariachis from Boston. 4) Each one of the family members wore expensive clothing related to a decade of the 60's, 70's, and 80's. 5) The room walls were decorated by gigantic vinyl blankets designed by professional graphic artists. They had photographs of my sister and other emblems. There were also many other decorations that cost a lot of money.

What a party and what pomp for a family of country folks! It was a family oriented meeting where the true joy and peace of the Lord was manifested in our thankful hearts for the unmatchable work of Christ. There were many

reasons to celebrate. Even though the primary reason was
the 50th birthday of Trinis, the festivities demonstrated
the unity that manifests in the Vargas family. Above all,
we celebrated the fact that we are all believers in Jesus
Christ and the powerful fact that we are saved by faith and
the grace of Jesus. You tell me, could there be any more
reasons necessary for a big celebration? When it was all
over, we observed that the gifts were few. We had worried
so much about organizing the giant party that we forgot
to buy a deserving gift. And so, my brother Carlos and I
gave Trinis and her husband Baldemar a trip on American
Airlines to San Juan, Puerto Rico, where they would take
a cruise in the Caribbean.

My dear reader, I want to clarify that I share all of this with
you with the purpose of showing you that "in Christ, you
can do it." There is a Christian music group called "El
Trio de Hoy" (The Trio of Today). In one of their greatest
songs they sing saying, "We are those who believe that
with the power of God you can, you can, you can…" For
the Vargas's, that has not come to be just a little chorus
with good music and a special rhythm, but it has become
a reality and a lifestyle. We believe that with the power of
God we can undertake great projects. We believe that God
does extraordinary things, with ordinary people. Some
could criticize our family reunions and our festivities, but
the truth is that we do it because God gives us the grace
to achieve it.

THE WEDDING OF MARK
AND LLUVIA

Allow me to finish this subject of great celebrations, by
telling you about the magnificent wedding of my son Mark
and Lluvia. I will do it in only eight to ten lines: We did

not have money, we did not have credit, but my son Mark dedicated himself to work hard and to have a lot of faith. Those two elements were so effective that the wedding was, until this day, the one with the greatest attendance. Once again we broke records. Nobody in our community in Rhode Island had celebrated a reception with such a high number of guests who showed up. We invited 560 people, of which 439 arrived. The cost of the reception in the blazing "Venus de Milo" was quite considerable, but, it was done. My young son summoned all his strength and before I tried to pay for something, he had already paid for everything. Glory to God once again! He allows his servants to celebrate his victories majestically.

8

A BIG TITLE FOR A SMALL SERVANT

"His clothing was strange; a camel skin robe with a leather belt. His food was strange: Locusts or grasshoppers and wild honey. His residence was uncomfortable: He lived in the desert, a place where nobody would like to live. He had no wife, no children, just a desert and a powerful message from God. He looked like a caveman, but was full of anointing. He challenged those Israelites to reconcile with God. The inhabitants of Judah went out to find him in the desolate areas, because that prophet spoke with authority. The people were moved at hearing the words he said because he told the truth, he challenged them to leave sin and be baptized as a sign of repentance. Hundreds responded to his call. The multitudes surrounded him even though he wasn't seeking to be the center of attention. He announced that the Messiah was soon to come, and that he would not be worthy to untie the cords of his sandals. In that time, the slaves removed the sandals of their masters and their guests when they arrived at a house, and washed their feet. This servant of God did not consider himself worthy to even be called a slave of Christ Jesus. He considered the title too lofty for him. Although when it came to spiritual authority, he spoke with boldness, telling the truth right to their face without caring who his listeners were. Because of this he also earned a lot of enemies, like Herod himself who finally killed him by decapitation. But of course, he could not kill the message, because that which this prophet announced, had already been set in motion since the beginning of all creation and even before; and it is the same now with His earthly ministry. It was precisely Jesus himself who gave the following opinion of him, *"Verily I say unto you, among them that are born of women there hath not risen a greater than John the Baptist: notwithstanding he that is least in the kingdom of heaven is greater than he"* (Matthew 11:11). The Lord of lords and King of kings gave him a lofty title, "The greatest of all the Prophets. However he considered himself to be the least worthy and the smallest servant of Jesus Christ."

Despite everything I have written up to now about my 45 years of "A Life of Miracles", even with that, with all sincerity and confidence I consider myself a minuscule servant of God. There is more, among all my colleagues and Christian communicators of mass media on the Continent, I feel that I am "the caveman" who is just now starting to learn how to behave myself; an ordinary man whom God has done extraordinary things through; a common man who has seen the supernatural hand of God in uncommon situations; finally, a man with virtues and defects. I am a repentant sinner, washed by the precious crimson blood that flowed from Calvary. I am a person of flesh and blood. Obviously, I am not a heavenly or angelic being. Although I do have my eyes on heaven, I have my feet on the ground. Notwithstanding, despite my smallness, the Lord has conceded the blessing of his power working in a marvelous and transcendental way. Among those great portents that have happened to me, even though I consider myself to be "the caveman of communication ," "the son of a country woman," "the kid born in the mountains," I was given a series of lofty titles.

In this final chapter, for the glory of God, I want to tell you about the triple vestments they gave me in a single day. That day was Saturday, April 17, 2010. That blessed and unforgettable day they conferred to me the following titles: 1) Apostle to the Nations, 2) Bishop for Shalom International Church Consortium, 3) Doctor of Philosophy in Ministry, Ph.D. Honoris Causa. I cannot be mistaken in saying they gave "a big title to a small servant." You, my dear reader, can also achieve big things for God, even if you feel unworthy, tiny or insignificant. God wants and can lift you up to the highest if you just dare to believe and give the glory to him.

Let me tell you, when I thought I had finished writing this book, I found myself with an email telling me that it wasn't really time to call it off. By the advice of the director of my writing staff, I have added this final chapter where I end the history of my life up to my current age of 45. I had never thought about it, but it's true that this work would be incomplete if I did not share with you something up to date. The Bible says that *"Jesus Christ the same yesterday, and today, and forever"* (Hebrews 13:8). In the way that he did miracles in my past, I would also like to prove that he continues doing them today and will continue tomorrow.

SURELY IT WAS A DREAM
OR MAYBE A VISITATION...

It was strange to me, because when my inauguration was organized and completed, I didn't hear any destructive criticism. I am so used to people complaining; those who bite the hand that feeds them and the negative comments, but this time I was waiting for them and they never came. Finally, their absence was eye-catching. I didn't know if I had broken through a barrier or a record, or maybe simply for the first time they were in favor of something about me.

For a long time I have executed the function of Bishop for hundreds of churches who throughout the years we have linked with, to work under my Ministerial Covering, and under my mentorship. About 50% of these congregations are Charismatic, Neo Pentecostals and Pentecostals; the remaining 50% are traditional, Baptists, Methodists, Presbyterians, etc., etc., etc. To me, that is more than a miracle, seeing as I have achieved that churches from distinct denominations focus on what unites us in Christ and not on denominational differences.

Although I never desired it, I was notified of it some 20 years ago by a divine person that visited me one night and wouldn't let me sleep, waking me up over and over again. He communicated to me that I would preside over many churches in many countries. Surely for some people it was a dream, although to me, it was much more than that, I consider it to be a divine visitation.

LORD, LET ME SLEEP

That was the first time something similar occurred to me. Years before, at the beginning of the development of my radio ministry, someone who I never saw with clarity, arrived when I was sleeping and woke me up with these words, "Brother Mynor, your radio programs have been approved in Venezuela." Immediately after I woke up the angel would disappear, but I would have that voice recorded in my mind and in my heart. When sleep overcame me, I would doze off, only to be almost immediately awakened with the same words, but there would be a change in the country, "Brother Mynor, your radio programs have been approved in Costa Rica." This happened dozens of times. Sometimes they would tell me, "The radio station networks in this country, approved your radio programs", or "the radio association in this other country, approved your radio program." The last thing I remember was that the light of the new dawn was pouring through my window. I was sweating rivers and was very tired. All night I had been awakened time after time. That was when I prayed and asked God to please let me sleep. Said and done, the celestial being did not wake me up again. The next day I could not concentrate on anything else and to this day I cannot forget that visitation. It happened at the beginning of my call to do international radio. It occurred to me when I didn't even know how to speak with a microphone... or without one.

Now, the second time that I had a similar visitation was approximately six years after the first. This visitor woke me over and over again interrupting my sleep throughout the whole night, and said to me, "Brother Mynor, the churches in this country have joined with you." I woke up surprised; I couldn't see anyone. I couldn't distinguish whether it was a dream, vision or reality. The only thing I was sure of was that the presence of God filled my room. Each time it woke me, it was in an almost violent and pressing way. I would sit abruptly in the bed. Another detail I remember is that the night was darker than ever. There was no soft light for me to see. The darkness was so dense, that when I woke up scared because of the voice I heard, "I could almost see" when the celestial being who spoke to me so authoritatively in the ear disappeared. Strange thing don't you think? I awoke again with very wet clothing because of the sweat, wishing to sleep. But this time I didn't want to pray that God would not speak more. I was afraid the angel or divine being would be grieved. So I resisted more or less the same amount of hours as the first time, until I was at the point of not being able to take it any longer. So again I prayed and asked God to please let me sleep and that if I did sleep, and nobody woke me up again, it would confirm that it was him who sent me a messenger and I would prepare myself for this great labor of supporting pastors and churches in the nations. Ladies and gentlemen, once again, "said and done", I slept peacefully until more or less 9 or 10 in the morning.

The next day, I myself could not believe what I had experienced the night before. That was the second time something like that had happened to me. Without any doubt, God called me to something grand and majestic, something that had not come into my heart before. The Bible says well, *"But as it is written, Eye hath not seen, nor ear heard, neither have entered into the heart of man, the things which God hath prepared for them that love him"* (1 Corinthians 2:9). I remember that I shared this testimony with about five close people almost immediately. I was already living in the "Cliff House" (Casa Cliff) where I live currently. There I called a corporate assembly. Two people were absent because they already had an idea of what I was going to say and they didn't believe it. One of them arrived to explain the reason why they didn't show up. Three of the invited, were present and I told them about the visitation. They all remained silent, there was not a single response other than from Pastor Victor Suchite, who in that time was my disciple and now is my colleague and International Advisor. Suchite told me, "I do believe you, and time will show how God will make that a reality." The interesting thing is that for me the time has now arrived at my age of 45. "The time" that Victor was talking about, has now arrived and I am now doing the work I did not ask for, or seek, but God put in my hands.

Faith takes us far, but faith only transports the people who dare to believe. Victor and I were the only ones who believed and, as a result, we are the only ones who remain part of the original team in this vision.

ME, A BISHOP?

I remember that I dealt with and talked about my doubts with several of my advisors, mentors, personal friends and even some of my most severe critics. I wanted to have a thousand opinions at hand before accepting vestment and Bishopric ordination. I asked them, "How is it possible that God has called me to do this?" Isn't there someone with more merit and preparation like this guy, that guy or the other guy (mentioning various mega pastors and mega ministers in the world)? I never believed even in the little bit, that I deserved such trust from God. I affirm that with ALL sincerity. The reason why I believe that is because I know myself; I know my limitations and my weaknesses. And so, I understand perfectly that there are people who are more capable, more faithful and worthy than I. However, in His sovereign will, it pleased God to give me this work which I am doing in obedience.

What I least imagined in my ministerial life, was to become a Bishop. I was always attracted to the Ministry of International Evangelist and Conference Speaker, but not the one that was related to the office of Bishop.

The Pastors from Rhode Island have given their opinion that this festivity and the ordination has been the biggest in the ecclesiastic history of the State. There were ministers there representing many different nations, from South America, Central America, the Caribbean, North America and Europe. Other servants of God did not attend because the announcement arrived at very short notice. However, we had people who were very interested in coming from Africa and Asia. Each person who was present gave a greater enhancement to that spiritual event. It was done for the glory of God and nobody came for their own honor, but they gave the glory to the Lord.

A TRIPLE VESTMENT

Among the distinguished visitors of that marvelous night, there was my admired friend and Soul Brother Dr. Harold Caballeros, the current presidential candidate for the Republic of Guatemala and founder of the mega church, El Shaddai. His dear wife Cecilia de Caballeros also attended, who is the current Senior Pastor of the El Shaddai Church. Also, forming part of the honorable cast was the Patriarch Norman Parish, one of the most respected elders in my country of Guatemala. Parish has been responsible directly or indirectly for the foundation of hundreds of churches in many countries. Dr. Ernest Gibson, President of Grace Christian University also arrived, as well as Dr. Michael Pangio, Chairman of Grace Christian University, respectively. They came personally to confer to me, a Ph.D. According to diverse encyclopedias a Doctor of Philosophy is a person that has received the last, most elevated and preeminent academic level conferred in a university. The title came to be my sixth doctorate degree in life. How ironic that a boy from the jungle became a six time doctor!

ALBERTO MOTTESI

Other than the aforementioned amazing guests who arrived that night, there was a letter that Lic. M.A. Victor Suchite would read which I never dreamed to receive. It came from Global Evangelist Alberto Mottesi, the minister who has been a model for my life and ministry. Alberto and his wife Nohemi expressed in this letter, that they were very sorry for not being able to be present because of a recent surgery. However, they sent their congratulations, and together with it was a giant "sword" as a trophy to honor my 28 years of ministry to the nations. It was "the sword of David." I could not categorize that as anything less than a dream come true. The recognition to me was like something "very big" for a "small servant." However, that distinguished and fiery evangelist was willing to send it to me, and to top it off, with a gold brooch, it was given to me in front of hundreds of people. I never imagined that the evangelist I most admired in my life, Alberto Mottesi, would extend recognition to me. Yes, to me, Mynor Vargas the boy from the mountains. Oh, glory to God in the highest and peace here on earth! I cannot do less than this, to stop from writing my story and start writing praise to God who loves us so much, who can do all things, and does all things, amen.

BROTHER PAUL

It also honored me a lot to receive two emails from the renowned Brother Paul (Hermano Pablo), who I consider to be my Ministerial Father and the man most dear to my life, in the ministerial aspect. Paul and Linda Finkenbinder are the model of integrity and holiness which Blanqui and I try to live by. Of course, I confess that we have not achieved the level they have achieved. However, we do what is possible, trying faithfully. I felt extremely nervous reading each one of those two emails from Brother Paul. I worried about the way my main Mentor and Ministerial Father would interpret the ordination. It so happens, that Brother Paul is so righteous in these situations that he prefers to avoid all presumption of titles. He takes care in that aspect, and opts to be called and known simply as "Brother Paul." Then here I come, someone who is not worthy to untie his shoes; and I accept being ordained not only the Bishop of the Shalom International Church Consortium, but in that same day be anointed as "Apostle to the Nations." If that wasn't enough, I agreed to receive from Grace Christian University the title of "Doctor of Philosophy in Ministry, Ph.D.."

As the father of Brother Paul used to say, "To eat with someone is to know someone." On many repeated occasions I have crossed the country of the United States of North America (from Boston to Los Angeles) just to go have dinner with Paul and Linda Finkenbinder. Exclusively, I have traveled on multiple occasions to be with them for a couple of hours in California. The purpose of these trips has been to arrive to a dinner with this distinguished Elder, to be taught by him, be blessed by his prayer throughout a couple of hours and then take a flight in route to my next mission. That is how we have both gotten to know each other dearly and we have linked our two ministerial hearts. Therefore, Brother Paul also knows perfectly well that I also do not seek titles, with the only difference that when someone gives them to me, I just say the words, "Your kingdom come, your will be done." The issue is that for me it was a high honor to know through those emails, that Brother Paul blessed my vestment and blessed my ordination with words and wise advice.

GALA AND SPLENDOR

That night the distinguished visitors were transported in a presidential black limousine. As a prelude to the service, the harp was played by Amy Hopkins as instrumental music to prepare the atmosphere. During the service, my niece Michelle Lima, surprised us all with a very stirring and inspiring dance. The local pastors dressed with gala in their best suits. Other servants of God came in priestly clothes and clerical collars. Those who had academic titles came in doctorate robes. The press and professional photographers used the sharpest technology. There was abundant food at the end of the service for all those present and many other surprises. Who could believe that night would be the celebration of a triple vestment of someone who 45 years before was at the point of not being born, someone who had a mountain waiting for him as a backyard, and a piece of moss covered wood as a walker to learn to take his first steps?...

EVERYONE WAS A V.I.P.

That night, everyone was declared a V.I.P. (Very Important Person). It was not a public event, but an exclusive gathering. Therefore, there were only about 470 people total. Approximately 350 of them in the main auditorium, some 55 serving and about 65 children with a team of pastors dressed as clowns.

Present was my first mentor, Pastor and Dr. Moises Mercedes, who traveled many long hours on the road, to be able to accompany me and anoint me with oil alongside the other servants.

My ordination was very honored by the diverse ministers and ministries represented. Among them was the President of the Fraternity of Pastors of Rhode Island, Reverend Eliseo Nogueras and his wife Ida Maldonado Nogueras. The Rev. Nogueras on several occasions has expressed elevated praise of me, saying, "If anyone is TRULY a Bishop and Apostle, it is Mynor Vargas. Mynor not only has the title, but he also has the churches and does the job." That was said by the President of the Fraternity of Pastors before the ordination, during and after. There were also members of the Coalition of Pastors of Rhode Island and members of the New England Coalition of Leaders and Christian Pastors and members of the Fraternity of Pastors of R.I. to close with splendor the event. There were also present a representation of ministers not allied with any of these organizations. Men and women of God who have opted in their free will to function independently, without belonging to any of these organizations, but they did opt to be part of my ordination. Glory to God!

THREE BIG TITLES WITHOUT DESERVING THEM

Today, without me seeking it, without asking for it or deserving it, I am the First Bishop of more than 600 churches on the 6 continents. Under my covering or ministerial support, there are pastors, bishops, apostles and other ministers. Moreover, I am the Founder and Director of the International Federation of Chaplains which has more than 1,800 men and women serving in 40 nations in the world. I can also now add the letters Ph.D. after my name, according to the academic level that has been conferred to me. After all that, I am still convincing myself that in the ministerial practice, I truly am a Bishop and I execute functions as an Apostle.

I say that because in the beginning it was difficult for me to accept the commission, the ordination and the anointing. It took me approximately three years to decide to allow said vestment to take place. To this day with all bravery I can affirm that I do not regret it, because the practice of anointing people for ministry is totally Biblical.

THE MIRACLES WILL HAVE TO KEEP TAKING PLACE

God is in control of the universe and our lives. We are only his servants. He does what seems best to him, in his sovereign will. I say this because I would like God to give me one BIG miracle above all that I need in my life, family and ministry and then not have to continue believing for each individual miracle. Which is to say, in terms of the finances I had mentioned, I would like God to give me all the millions that I need and then just be able to take out of it each time I need money. But, "A Life of Miracles" doesn't work that way. God prefers that we continue close to him in constant prayer and dependence, so it won't be that once he gives us everything at one time, we forget about his power and divine dependence. It is for that reason that I understand that "the miracles will have to keep happening", because needs will keep coming up. In the model prayer, Jesus asked, *"Give us this day our daily bread"* (Matthew 6:11). I don't ask for bread for a week, or for a month, and less for my whole life. I ask for the food for each day, I don't ask for a pantry full of food. If God were to give us everything together, we would surely forget about him and we would not seek him daily in prayer!

I want to leave it clear that life is not easy. Jesus himself warned us, *"In the world ye shall have tribulation: but be of good cheer; I have overcome the world"* (John 16:33). Because of that, in our moments of adversity we must exercise our faith and trust that God will be attentive to manifest a miracle in the midst of need. As I write this final part of my autobiography, I am still 45 years old and at the point of turning 46. When this book is printed and finally arrives in your hands, I will be at least 46 or more years. At that age, I can affirm that I am living a very pleasant and exciting stage in my life. I invest equivalently my time in "living for me", "living for my family" and "living for the ministry." As I feel that I am becoming more of a veteran or mature, I see more how God confirms his mercy and calling on my life. I can say that I live as a Christian song says, "Circumstances don't move me, the victorious one lives in me." Why do I mention that? Because as I write these last lines of my autobiography, I am going through serious financial difficulties, and I confirm that that life of miracles does not guarantee a peaceful flight, but it **does guarantee you will land!**

Without a doubt, the recession we are living through in the United States, and in the rest of the world, has been the cause of many ministries going through financial crisis. However, I see an opportunity in the midst of the crisis, the opportunity to believe in God, the opportunity to receive a miracle. Faith is like a bridge. Each time you are in front of an abyss, there are two options: Pass over the bridge of faith or fall into the depths of the gorge. On my part, once again I am confident and serene. As the miracle arrives, I can sing or at least hum the beautiful song of my friend Juan Carlos Alvarado, whose first verse says, "God will make trails where there are none. He will work in ways we don't understand. He will guide me. At his side I will be. He will give me love and strength. A trail he will make where there are none." Without a doubt, that fills us with faith.

So I leave that situation pending to know that God will work and I will testify of it in my next book. I will concentrate now on telling how God has been big and powerful in this year 2010 when I close four decades and a half of life on this beautiful planet Earth.

THE LAST MIRACLE

The last miracle can only be described as this book arriving in your hands, because as I write it, I don't have the money or sponsors to complete the costs of publication. I confess including, I still have to pay my editors and translators a good sum of money. However, the peace and faith which governs my heart assures me that within a few months, you will be reading comfortably this book of faith.

FINAL WORDS

I would like to be flooded with emails. I would like you to tell me in what way "A Life of Miracles" has blessed your life, your family and your ministry. Tell me the way in which the Biblical foundations I presented to you and the personal testimonies helped you to achieve your miracle for yourself. Remember that this book was written thinking of you. I have lived a lot of miracles and I assure you that I will continue living them. Now it is your turn, YES, YOUR TURN, MY BELOVED FRIEND, dare to believe. Dare and voyage to your miracle. Do it today in the name of Jesus, amen.

<u>Christian Chaplain Certificate in 30 Days</u>

For Pastors, Ministers and Leaders with more than 5 years' experience. Obtain the credentials that will open many doors. Currently our Federation is active with more than 2,000 Certified Christian Chaplains in more than 40 countries and 6 continents. Glory to God!
FOR MORE INFORMATION.
VISIT TODAY

www.ChaplainFederation.com

<u>Obtain your Doctorate in Divinity</u>
FAST!

Study Theology and Ministry with our University.

Crown Theological Seminary of New England offers an
articulate and concise curriculum which can be studied
100% over the internet and completed FAST as you
continue exercising your ministry or current office.
FOR MORE INFORMATION.
VISIT TODAY

www.CrownSeminary.org

International Consortium of Shalom Churches
COVERING WITHOUT PRESSURE!!!

Doctor Mynor Vargas knows the needs that Pastors and Ministers face daily. His ministry as the Bishop of the Consortium and Apostle to the nations is more than a title; it is an office that he performs daily in an effective way in favor of the Pastors and Ministers under his ministerial and professional covering.
FOR MORE INFORMATION.
VISIT TODAY
www.ShalomRI.com

Made in the USA
Middletown, DE
07 September 2023

37735956R00116